COSTA BRAVA

By the staff of Editions Berlitz

Library of Congress Catalog Card Number:
76-21361.

Berlitz Trademark Reg. U.S. Patent Office
and other countries – Marca Registrada.

Printed in Switzerland by Weber SA, Bienne

Revised edition 1981

COSTA
BRAVA

Preface

A new kind of travel guide for the jet age. Berlitz has packed all you need to know about the Costa Brava into this compact and colourful book, one of an extensive series on the world's top tourist spots.

Like our phrase books and dictionaries, this book fits your pocket—in both size and price. It also aims to fit your travel needs:

- It concentrates on your specific destination—the Costa Brava —not an entire country.

- It combines easy reading with fast facts; what to see and do, where to shop, what to eat.

- An authoritative A-to-Z "blueprint" fills the back of the book, giving clear-cut answers to all your questions, from "When are the banking hours?" to "How much does a haircut cost?" —plus how to get there, when to go and what to budget for.

- Easy-to-read maps in full colour of the region pin-point sights you'll want to see.

In short, this handy guide will enhance your enjoyment of the Costa Brava and Catalonia. From the colourful market town of Torroella to the wild beauty of the 10th-century Monastery of San Pedro de Roda in the Pyrenean foothills, from the broad sandy beaches of Palamós to the exciting folk dances at the annual festival of San Feliú de Guixols, Berlitz tells you clearly and concisely what it's all about.

Let your travel agent help you choose a hotel.
Let a restaurant guide help you find a good place to eat.
But to decide "What should we do today?" travel with Berlitz.

Area specialist and photographer: Ken Welsh.
We wish to thank the Spanish National Tourist Office, particularly Miss Mercedes Martín Bartolomé, for their valuable assistance.

4 🐦 Cartography: Falk-Verlag, Hamburg.

Contents

Maps: Bird's Eye-View of Costa Brava pp. 6–7, Costa Brava pp. 18–19, Port Bou–Ampuriabrava p. 25, La Escala–Palamós p. 32, Palamós–Blanes p. 44, Gerona Old City p. 54, From Gerona to Andorra p. 60, Central Barcelona p. 60.

How to use this guide

If time is short, look for items to visit which are printed in bold type in this book, e.g. **Peratallada.** Those sights most highly recommended are not only given in bold type, but also carry our traveller symbol, e.g. **Gerona.**

The Costa Brava and the Catalans

If ever one small part of the planet was blessed with everything, this is surely it. Facing the Mediterranean, flanked to the north by the mighty Pyrenees, the Costa Brava offers sandy beaches, hidden coves, offshore islands, charming fishing villages, imposing castles with a backdrop of magnificent mountains and a first-rate climate. It forms part of the Catalonian province of Gerona, and is a region of history and art, of cathedrals and achievements, of alternately lush and harsh scenery and, to top it all, the best skiing in Spain.

To the seafaring Catalans, this particular strip of the coast was always known as *brava,* a term with a whole range of meanings: wild, savage, dangerous, craggy, stormy, steep. But it was the Catalan poet, Ferrán Agulló, who,

in 1908, first officially coined the name for the coast as a geographical entity running from Banyuls (just over the border in France) down to the estuary of the Tordera.

To find out just how wild, geographically speaking, the Costa Brava is, take an hour's drive around the hairpin bends above the cliffs of the northern or southern extremes of the coast. And even then you've only had a glimpse; the rest is hidden...

A droll little Gerona joke asks, "In how many countries of the world do they speak Spanish?" Answer: "Well, now, they speak it in Galicia, the Basque country, in Catalonia..." A very wry joke, but it helps to explain Spain's fascination. For Spain is many nations under one flag, and Catalonia is one of them.

Spanish is, in fact, one of two languages spoken in Catalonia. The people of Gerona, and the other three provinces of Catalonia, are bilingual. They speak Catalan, a derivative of Latin, along with (and often better than) the official language of Spain, Castilian. Catalan or its dialects are spoken from the French Pyrenees to Valencia, in the Balearic Islands and, surprisingly, in parts of Sardinia—a reminder

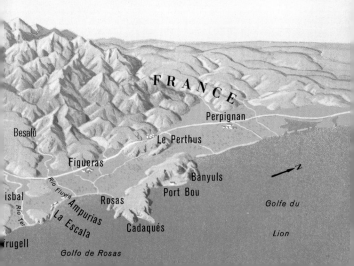

of Catalonia's great medieval kingdom. Ironically, Catalan is the *official* language of only one country—Andorra.

You'll often be reminded that the Catalans are a race apart, as different from the Andalusians or Basques as the Welsh and Scots are from the English. They are acutely aware of their own history and culture.

Unlike the Spanish stereotype, the Catalans are dynamic, canny and industrious. This may account for their reputation elsewhere in Spain as mercenary and uncompromising. Catalonia's best reply is the roster of outstanding artists who have emerged during a century desperately short of talent in other parts of the country. Caught between the two worlds of Europe and Iberia, Catalonia has been

able to absorb the best of both and produce giants such as Joan Miró, Salvador Dalí and, something of an adopted son, Picasso. In architecture the genius was Gaudí; in music, Casals.

Music is important in the lives of the Catalans. They sing in choirs, play in bands and dance the *sardana*. This gracious, courtly dance is as essentially Catalan as flamenco is Andalusian. And it is a living part of the culture, not a folklore oddity dragged out of the cupboard to entertain the tourists. The *sardana* bridges the generation gap; young and old join hands to dance it every week in resorts up and down the Costa Brava.

"People interpret the closed circle of the *sardana* as a symbol of our unity *against* the outside world," goes the Catalan explanation. "But if anyone, even a foreigner, touches the circle, it opens to accept him. *That* is a symbol of our willingness to embrace anyone who attempts to understand us."

Your desire to understand the Catalans—if not necessarily to be embraced by them—can only be heightened by the dramatic surroundings of the Costa Brava. But as you enjoy their scenery and hearty food and wine, as you tour their archaeological wonders and religious shrines, as you take advantage of the sports and nightlife and shopping... try not to envy them. After all, they were here first.

Left: *Old stones and lazy hound in Peratallada show town's easy pace. Typical feature of the Costa Brava is its jagged coastline (beware of twisting roads), as here near Tossa.*

A Brief History

Beneath the stone, sand and soil of the Costa Brava lurks the treasure of history. Digging, scraping and deducing, archaeologists have pieced together a new insight into Catalonia's ancient heritage.

Their most dramatic success has been the excavation of twin Greek and Roman cities at Ampurias, where the Greeks had set up a very important trading post. Another impressive discovery, inland from Estartit, revealed a 5th-century B.C. Celtiberian city at Ullestret.

The Celtiberians were the descendants of northern Celtic tribes who invaded the peninsula and settled down with the earlier arrivals, the Iberians.

Though several Mediterranean peoples traded and colonized on Spain's shores, the first to make any real impact on Spanish history were the ambitious and warlike Carthaginians, arch-rivals of the Romans for Mediterranean supremacy. Hannibal, the military genius of Carthage, saw Catalonia as the gateway to victory. He marched his elephants through Gerona Province as he prepared to invade Rome during the Second Punic War, but failed, and Rome enfolded Spain into its ever-expanding empire. The brave Celtiberians resisted for two whole centuries, but around 20 B.C., the last part of the peninsula (Galicia) was finally subdued and declared a Roman province.

Rome brought political stability and an advanced culture to Spain. During the six centuries of occupation, the Romans built cities and roads, inaugurated government and law, and provided the base for the Spanish and Catalan languages. The colony, in turn, made its contribution to the thriving civilization of Rome: the philosopher Seneca, the poet Martial and the emperors Trajan and Hadrian, all were born in Spain.

But as the unwieldy empire entered its decline, successive waves of intruders chipped away at the Roman edifice. Spain was overrun by Vandals and Visigoths. Corruption and intrigue in the 300-year Visigothic occupation left the kingdom defenceless in the face of Spain's most momentous event.

In A.D. 711, the Moors of North Africa invaded across the Straits of Gibraltar. They defeated the Visigothic defenders at Tarifa and within ten years had conquered most of the country. Then, crossing the Pyrenees, they pushed into France until the Frankish general, Charles Martel, turned them back at Poitiers in 732.

The Moors installed their religion and culture in Spain, but Christian resistance never died. The battle to expel Islam see-sawed for centuries before

The 'Catholic Monarchs' Ferdinand and Isabella united Spain in 1492.

the ultimate triumph of the Catholic Monarchs, Ferdinand and Isabella.

In the early stages of the struggle, Charlemagne, the Frankish warrior-king, expelled the Moors from Gerona and Barcelona. He integrated these territories into what was called the Spanish March, a buffer zone between the Christian and Muslim power bases.

The first hero of Catalonia emerged in a skirmish between the Frankish forces and the Moors. His name was Wifredo el Velloso (Guifredo Pelio in Catalan), meaning Wilfred the Hairy. The noble Wilfred threw his support behind a Frankish king who was his opposite number in more ways

The 10th-century Monastery of San Pedro de Roda, north Costa Brava, was an important religious centre.

than one, Charles the Bald. When Wilfred fell wounded, the legend goes, the king asked what reward he desired. The request—independence for Barcelona— was granted. The year was 878.

The Golden Age

In the Middle Ages, Catalonia became strong commercially, politically and intellectually. Count Ramón Berenguer I of Barcelona drew up a sort of constitution, the *Usatges,* in 1060. Ramón Berenguer III (1096–1131) expanded trade alliances. But the Berenguer dynasty's greatest coup took place at the church altar when Ramón IV (1131–62) married the daughter of the King of Aragon, creating the joint kingdom of Catalonia and Aragon.

In Catalonia's heyday, the combined Crown was scarcely challenged in the Mediterranean. At one time Catalonia controlled outposts in Greece, Italy, Sicily, Sardinia and Corsica. Shipyards worked overtime to expand the Catalan merchant fleet; the Crown wrote a code of maritime law; and an enterprising group of merchants founded a marine insurance company.

Conquest—more economic than military—was by no means everything. This was the era of great architecture and art: original churches with vast naves and tall, slim columns and the astonishing sculptures and paintings which glorified them. And Catalonia's scholars and philosophers prospered.

The most significant nuptials in three centuries united Ferdinand, Prince of Aragon, and Isabella of Castile in 1469. Their combined kingdom began the final conquest of the tenacious Moors, culminating in the capture of Granada in 1492. The Catholic Monarchs supervised two other historic events of the same year. They expelled the Jews from Spain. And they sent Columbus on his voyage to America.

The Columbus project and other adventures far afield had ironic effects on Catalonia. As Spain entered its Golden Age, all eyes now turned to the wealth of the New World, stripping the Mediterranean trade routes of much of their importance. And, in the inter-province rivalries, the Catalonians found themselves relegated to a second-class position in favour of Castile. Catalans were even forbidden access to the New World territories. The great new commercial centres were Cádiz and Seville. **13**

Times of Troubles

The uncountable riches the Conquistadors shipped home from America drastically strengthened Spain's position in European politics. But the seeds of disaster were planted. Spain's gold drained away in endless wars in Italy and Holland. The demoralizing defeat of the Invincible Armada in 1588 brought further ruin. Each military adventure and each new king seemed worse than the last.

In Catalonia, the discontent seethed against Philip IV, flaming into open rebellion in 1640. Louis XIII of France accommodatingly recognized the region as an independent state. The revolt of the Catalans raged for more than a decade. Spain won. In defeat, Catalonia managed to preserve its treasured local laws, but under allegiance to the Spanish Crown.

In the War of the Spanish Succession—really a struggle between France and the rest of Europe—Catalonia sided with

Gerona's medieval walls helped to defend city against many a siege.

the loser, Archduke Charles of Austria. Battles flared, cities were besieged. With the triumph of the Bourbon king, Philip V, the Catalonians were punished once more. The parliament was disbanded, and the Catalan language was banned from official use.

Along with the rest of Spain, Catalonia counted as little more than a satellite of France.

In the Peninsular War of 1808–14, which the Spaniards call the War of Independence, Catalonia fared badly yet again. The French quickly conquered Barcelona, but Gerona underwent a nine-month siege. A French army of 35,000 finally breached the walls of the starving city with mines. Eventually, with the aid of their new British allies led by the Duke of Wellington, Spain won its independence.

The legitimate monarchy may have been restored, but Spain now plunged headlong into a century of disastrous power struggles. Overseas, Spain's American colonies revolted and gained independence. The last Spanish possessions—Cuba, Puerto Rico and the Philippines—were eventually lost when the Americans intervened in the year 1898.

Following an embarrassing defeat by local rebels in Morocco, Alfonso XIII, in 1923, accepted a general, Primo de Rivera, as dictator of Spain. Six years later the general fell. Neither reform nor maintenance of order seemed possible. In 1931, the king himself went into exile as anti-royalist sentiment grew.

National elections favoured the Republicans, who advocated Socialist and anti-clerical policies. As conservative resistence began to crystallize, Catalonia was proclaimed an autonomous republic. This was the first time in more than two centuries that home rule had been achieved.

The Civil War

Confusion and disorder were growing in Spain. The conflict between left and right became more irreconcilable. Spain's youngest general, Francisco Franco, came to the head of a military insurrection in 1936. The whole world watched the three-year struggle; outside forces helped to prolong it. Franco, with the Nationalists, Falangists and Monarchists, could call upon the tanks and planes of Germany and Italy. The Republicans, a shaky coalition of Socialists, Communists and Anarchists, received help from Moscow and the volunteer International Brigades.

Military reverses forced the Republicans to move their capital from Valencia to Barcelona in late 1937, where there had already been an outbreak of bitter fighting be- **15**

tween two factions of the Republican side, Anarchists and Communists. There followed repeated bombings of Barcelona by Italian planes based on Majorca and a year of hardship for the population. The city fell at last in January, 1939, and Catalonia was again absorbed into Spain—four provinces out of the nation's 50. Within two months, the Civil War, in which not far from half a million Spaniards were killed, was over.

Modern Times

The neutrality of Spain in the Second World War enabled it to heal its wounds. In 1955 the country was admitted to the United Nations. The subsequent tourist invasion had profound effects on the economy and on the people. On Franco's death in 1975, King Juan Carlos I was crowned. Under his reign—and in spite of big problems—various regions including Catalonia have moved towards autonomy, and demo-

Going about day-to-day tasks in a typical old Catalonian village. Right: Winding roads of Pyrenean foothills hug coast by Port Bou.

cratic structures have been evolved, opening the way to membership in the Common Market and bringing Spain into the mainstream of Western European life.

Low prices are less a magnet than they were to tourists; visitors that come, however, find Spain's perennial qualities—beauty, fine climate, warm welcome—as abundant and attractive as ever.

Where to Go

To most Spaniards, the Costa Brava begins in Blanes north of Barcelona and ends at Port Bou on the French frontier; but to most outsiders it's the other way round, so we begin our survey heading south from the French border, with short inland excursions where desirable.

The Northern Reach

Where Spain meets France, the formidable Pyrenees roll down to meet the sea, and one of the most spectacular coastlines of the whole Mediterranean begins: nearly 125 miles of dramatic cliffs, hidden coves, a myriad of villages interspersed with broad and sandy beaches.

Little wonder that the Costa Brava has earned such a reputation: a pure blue sea barely ruffled by a few white specks, seen against a protective green wall of huge pines, perfectly shaped like open umbrellas and contrasting with the ochre earth. Gnarled olive trees, with its characteristic tall shoot in the middle, and the tortuous cork

COSTA BRAVA

trees add to the extraordinary symphony of colour.

Hunched round a small bay below the lonely frontier post lies PORT BOU,* a fishing village which enjoyed a brief period of notoriety early this century as a haven for smugglers coming and going between France and Spain. A strait-laced border town now, it is fondly remembered by countless motorists as their first taste of Spain—and perhaps their first swim in the pretty CALA PETITA.

Southwards the road twists and turns like tangled string threading its way through the

* Many place-names in Catalonia create spelling problems. In this book we avoid pedantic or nationalistic passions and spell the towns as they're most often listed on road signs and local maps. Either form, Castilian or Catalan, will be instantly recognizable.

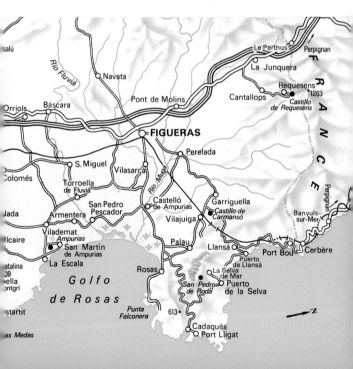

Pyrenean foothills until a dozen long kilometres later it finds LLANSÁ, now almost joined to its port, Puerto de Llansá. This quiet bay with its scorched and barren mountain backdrop was famed in particular for its rugged fishermen –said to be most skilful on the whole Brava coast—and for its tasty wines.

As so often on the Costa Brava, town and port were in former times separate, for Llansá, a thriving commercial harbour exporting wine and olives to France and Italy, was constantly being attacked by pirates. The town also developed a prosperous marble industry. Today, however, it is in the import business, enticing sun-starved Northerners to come and enjoy the delights of its beaches. Facing north, it is slightly cooler in summer than the rest of the Costa Brava, and its quarter mile of shingly beach and the shallow waters attract many tourists in search of peace and quiet.

Naked hills shield **Puerto de la Selva** (8 km. beyond) from icy winds (the *tramontana*) whipping down from the Pyrenees in winter. But these same hills were once so densely wooded (the name means "port of the woods") that the only easy access was by sea.

This natural protection offered safety to prehistoric communities; flint knives, pottery and over 70 Iron Age graves have been unearthed in the area around Punta del Pi.

A few treacherous motorcraft have crept in among the fishing boats in the pretty natural port, closed in by the dock. The town's site, clustered round its bay and protected by the towering mountains behind, inspires its reputation as the capital of this northern stretch of the Costa Brava.

As with Llansá, Puerto de la Selva has its "twin" town 2 kilometres inland. LA SELVA DE MAR huddles in a small valley not visible from the sea, and its main activity used to be farming; its port grew up later when the danger of pirate attacks had abated. Apart from its charm, La Selva de Mar serves as departure point for the **Monastery of San Pedro de Roda.**

Two hours' hard walking takes a visitor to the top of bleak Mount Vedera (over 2,000 feet); you won't regret your exertions when you see the impressive ruins of a 10th-century fortified monastery. Benedictine monks enlarged it and reconstructed existing foundations to make this the most influential ecclesiastical centre in the region.

This landmark of Catalonian Romanesque architecture, abandoned in the 18th century, is being extensively restored. The noble monastery, set against the arid landscape with the sea and Puerto de la Selva far below, makes an unforgettable sight.

Mount Vedera, the last Pyrenean foothill to reach the coast, also provides a suitably mysterious setting for ruins of the Castillo de San Salvador (Castle of the Holy Saviour).

For those who prefer to come by car, a difficult road of bumps and potholes leaves from VILAJUIGA, 9 kilometres away.

Plenty of fun and sun for all on town beach at Puerto de la Selva.

✤ Cadaqués

If Puerto de la Selva is "capital" of the northern reaches of the Costa Brava and Rosas that of the southern stretch, Cadaqués rules in splendid isolation over the Peninsula of Cabo de Creus to the east.

The road linking Puerto de la Selva with Cadaqués, 12 kilometres away, is wearying, with few signs of life or even vegetation. Yet Cadaqués is

one of the most hospitable and picturesque of all the spots on the Costa Brava.

Coming as it does at the end of an intense, desolate drive, the sudden sight of this charming town is something of a miracle. On a steep hillside, dazzling white houses with red roofs climb towards the massive church through straggling cobbled alleyways. At the harbour, cafés and restaurants beside the promenade look over the small bay where a few fishing boats keep up the image of a fishing village while water-skiers perform in front.

Cadaqués has had a long, eventful history, marked in particular by pirate raids, which has no doubt given the people their reputation as indomitable characters, self-assured and independent (and the coast's most skilful smugglers). The worst raid of all came with Barbarrossa (Red Beard), who in 1543 sacked the town and burned the original church. The present church, built in the 17th century, has a remarkable Baroque altarpiece by Pedro Costa.

Other regular invaders were the French; in 1285, the town recorded its first French intrusion and during the Peninsular War, its last (official) one. But even today Cadaqués is invaded every summer by the French, along with holiday-makers of a dozen nationalities. They tend to return regularly, swearing that this town with its pleasant rhythm of life and exceptionally clear light is the prettiest of all; one only has to see the number of easels planted everywhere to realize that it is a real artist's town.

The fame of Cadaqués has certainly been enhanced by the reputation and antics of the surrealist painter Salvador Dalí and his wife Gala, who settled in 1929 in **Port Lligat**,

2 kilometres beyond Cadaqués. In that year, Dalí bought a one-roomed fisherman's house. Since then, he has bought adjoining houses and redesigned them for the attractive Daliesque enclave to be seen down by the port today.

Many of Dalí's works uncannily reflect the pervading spirit of this strange region. "Here", he once said, "the mornings are of a savage and bitter gaiety and the evenings are often tinged with a morbid melancholy". Much of the jagged coastline is difficult to reach except by boat. Cadaqués itself and the road running round the bay are often choked with cars.

Cadaqués, with its dazzling white houses, rules in splendid solitude over the Cabo de Creus Peninsula.

Rosas

On the southern part of the Cabo de Creus, at Rosas, 15 kilometres beyond Cadaqués, begins a new type of Costa Brava: hospitable horizons, long, open beaches, expanses of flat country and the fertile Ampurdán plain behind. Rosas, from its original nucleus on the peninsula, spreads every year further down the lovely curve of the Golfo de Rosas, offering mile after mile of gently sloping sandy beaches. The setting is superb: on one side, the bay with its incredibly blue waters and, in the background, the lofty Pyrenees, at their most beautiful in winter and spring when the sun glitters on the snow on the peaks and reflects off the deep blue sea. It had long been a coastal favourite of the inhabitants of Figueras, 18 kilometres inland; the seemingly unending apartment blocks testify to its success.

Its popularity isn't new. The Greeks set up a trading post here (some claim that the name Rosas comes from Rhodes) and even earlier megalithic monuments have been found at Creu d'en Cobertella. From Rosas in 1354, in Catalonia's heyday, a fleet of 300 ships set sail to quell a revolt in Sardinia. In the 14th century, the town grew rich on the coral trade, and in 1543 Charles I built the massive, star-shaped fortress, La Ciudadela, as a measure against marauders. Despite this precaution, during the Peninsular War Rosas was taken by the French, who dismantled its fortifications piece by piece; you can still see the ruins today.

Rosas is famous for more than its outstanding beaches: thanks to the contortions of the coast's geography, the **port** faces due west; it has the most glorious sunsets on the whole Costa Brava. The reflection of the setting sun in the windows of the town is a memorable sight, with the distant peaks of the Garrotxa range beyond bathed in orange and red.

Not to be missed either is the arrival at about 6 in the evening of the fishing fleet, still a mainstay of the local economy. The return of the *vaques* to the perfect natural harbour formed by the Bay of Rosas never fails to move a visitor. Watch them auction the seafood on little round trays (the fish here are some of the tastiest on the whole coast).

If you find the long, flat beach too unexciting and require more adventurous

Lone sailing boat on a placid sea adds to dramatic sunset off Rosas.

bathing, explore the coastline to the north of Rosas—one intriguing *cala* (cove) after another.

Eight kilometres outside Rosas lies the large new residential and holiday complex of AMPURIABRAVA, set off between the Rivers Mugeta and Salinas. To many—but not all—it is the successful realization of the concept of an integrated holiday centre, incorporating facilities for all seaside and other outdoor activities, in a harmonious architectural ensemble. A maritime promenade skirts a fine white beach over a mile long. There's a yacht harbour and underwater-fishing club, and boat-supply shops with everything any skipper could want. A network of canals leads inland so that boats can be moored at the backdoor of the more luxurious quayside homes. The housing is low-key and cubic. Hotels, shopping centres, an observation tower (mirador), a shooting range, discotheques, tennis courts, an aero-club with its airfield—these are just a sample of what's to be found—plus the fine bathing on the beach in front.

Inland from Rosas

In this low-lying coastal area, the sea has abandoned some towns, leaving them high and dry when the region silted up. CASTELLÓ DE AMPURIAS is a case of a stranded town on a small rise just off the main road to Figueras, and 5 kilometres inland from Ampuriabrava.

Surrounded on all sides by

"tourist towns", it is as though tourism had never been heard of in Castelló de Ampurias. A look at the 14th-century **Gothic church** with its remarkable porch and statues of the 12 apostles is enough to suggest that this was a town of some importance. It was the capital of the whole neighbourhood and seat of the Counts of Ampurias. The really magnificent church, its vast forecourt, the old cobbled streets, the *Lonja* (old Stock Exchange) and the whole feel of the town remind one of its former opulence. It's all a delightful contrast to the modern coastal villages and developments.

According to records, PERELADA (8 kilometres further inland) was founded in the 9th century and its castle built in the 16th century; and, as things look today, very little has changed since then. The castle was the home of the Counts of Perelada for 400 years, but it serves quite a different purpose today: it has been converted into a casino, one of several in the area.

Another claim to fame: Ramón Muntaner, the 13th-century chronicler and war correspondent who covered the military exploits of the Catalans at the peak of their power, came from Perelada.

But in spite of all this, it is something else that draws flocks to Perelada. If it seems to you that people are reeling strangely, there's an easy explanation: Perelada is famed for its outstanding sparkling

Traffic ban in Rosas's main street is a boon to shoppers and strollers.

white wine, called locally *champán*. The invitation to visit the cellar to sample the sparkling cool wine can go to your head. Otherwise, have a taste of the refreshing drink at the big café near the entrance to the village—it's a few pesetas a glass! (Elsewhere you may have to buy a full bottle.)

LA JUNQUERA is Spain's busiest and best known frontier town, although it lies 6 kilometres from the actual border and is bypassed by the main road. It carries on its own happy existence and ignores the million cars passing in each direction annually in Northern Europe's Iberian summer migration. It has some pleasant houses and a 15th-century church. Nearby **Requesens Castle,** 12 kilometres up a bumpy road through Cantallops, was La Junquera's frontier sentinel.

Figueras

Figueras, 18 kilometres from Rosas, is Gerona Province's second largest town. So many visitors stop here for a last shopping spree before continuing up to La Junquera, the frontier, that the centre of the town gives an impression of being one gigantic market. Austere San Fernando Castle,

sitting squarely on the hill behind, is not open to the public. Begun in 1743, this military monolith has a girth of over 1 mile, and room enough for 10,000 men and 5,000 horses.

If Figueras has few pretentions to beauty, there is a great deal of character in the maze of back streets off the central *Ramblas* (promenade), where something is always going on—*sardanas*, exhibitions, or simply the hubbub and excitement in the packed cafés.

But it also has more serious claims to pride. First among them is Salvador Dalí, for the artist was born here, and since 1973 the town's main artistic attraction has been the amazing **Teatro-Museo Dalí.**

Castles in Spain

There are 5,000 officially classified castles in the land; some are magnificently preserved or restored (as the fairy-tale Alcázar at Segovia), while others are unidentifiable piles of rubble. During the Reconquest, 10,000 castles, fortified monasteries and farmhouses dotted the landscape as Spaniards poured their energies into the 700-year-long struggle to push back the Moors. So many were there in central Spain that the region to this day is known as *Castilla* (land of castles) and its inhabitants as *Castellanos* (castle-keepers).

Many Spanish castles are privately owned. If you'd like one yourself, write to Asociación Española de Amigos de los Castillos, located at Calle de Bárbara de Braganza, 8, Madrid. They may know of one for sale. Recently, castles have sold for as little as $3,750. The only trouble is that the repairs might run to as much as $100,000!

Within the maze of streets of the town centre, in the middle of a bare, red-tiled square and beside the very staid Church of San Pedro, you'll come upon a tortured tree trunk draped in a sheet and topped by some stones and a golden egg. Behind is the imposing façade of the building—a real theatre in the heyday of the town—and you realize you have arrived.

Everybody seems to have an opinion on Dalí, who on his own authority is The World's Greatest Painter. Make up your own mind on the ques-

tion as you tour this theatre-museum. Circus-ring ushers stand round as part of the décor in this extravagant monument Dalí created to his own ego. Beneath a great cupola ceiling, huge feet appear to be descending on the unwary visitor. In the Mae West Room, a deforming mir-

Modified Cadillac is a showpiece in Figueras's Salvador Dalí Museum.

Fishermen at San Pedro Pescador—Costa Brava's inland fishing port.

ror slung beneath the belly of a stuffed camel dissolves the view of a roomful of furniture into a seemingly three-dimensional portrait of the actress. A Cadillac parked in the patio has a large stone on its roof and a gilt-breasted amazon aforefront. In the curious setting of the theatre, the whole range of Dalí's creation—from the most "conventionally surrealist" to the wildest of his fantasies—can be seen, touched or activated, while all around, animated discussions are heard, punctuated by cries of hilarity—or admiration.

With the same ticket, you can visit the spick-and-span **Museo del Ampurdán** (Ampurdán Museum) on the Ramblas, dedicated to the history of the region and in quite another vein from the last museum. It takes us from Greek and Roman objects to the present day via pottery, woodcarvings, portraits of local notables, landscape paintings and folk art. Picasso, Miró (who dedicated a work to the museum) and (predictably) Dalí are represented.

Just opposite the museum on the central square, framed by the Ramblas, stands a statue of Narciso Monturiol (1819–85), who was the local hero (until eclipsed by Dalí). His invention, the wooden submarine, *Ictíneo,* operated manually by a crew of six, slid into Barcelona harbour in mid-summer 1861—a pioneering triumph of the era. The event went unnoticed by the outside world.

The Coast from Rosas to Palamós

San Pedro Pescador is an oddity for the Costa Brava: a fishing village with fishing boats but without sea. It lies on the banks of the River Fluviá, some 3 kilometres from the sea itself—all of which gives an incongruous if delightfully different air to this working fishing community set in an area which is mostly devoted to agriculture.

The safe inland position that protected San Pedro in the old days has disqualified it for entry into the 20th-century tourist stakes, but allowed it to preserve its real soul. While here, you may wish to make the journey to SAN MIGUEL DE FLUVIÁ, with its remarkable 11th-century Romanesque church.

LA ESCALA, a few miles down the coast at the southern end of the Gulf of Rosas, is deservedly an up-and-coming resort. A simple, typical fishing town until recently, its steep and animated streets lead down to a pretty harbour rimmed with waterfront bars and restaurants. The tourists share the beach space with boats, beside which fishermen sit mending their nets. A broad coastal road spans the whole town, but the usual local parking problems persist. Favourite swimming beaches are RIELLS and MONGÓ, several kilometres to the south.

La Escala (meaning the stopping place) was a halt on Hannibal's route north. The area is full of historical landmarks, and bathers who appreciate history will surely take a dip below SAN MARTÍN DE AMPURIAS, with its long, uncluttered, sandy beach. Here, just north of La Escala, sprawls the most remarkable archaeological site on the Costa Brava—the **ruins of Ampurias,** right beside the beach and with some last vestiges in the sea itself.

In the 6th century B.C., San Martín de Ampurias was a small island. Greek settlers built a port on the island that came to be known as Palaeopolis (the old city). Not long afterwards, they constructed another port, later called Neapolis (the new city), on the mainland a few hundred yards away. When the Romans came, they extended the whole complex and called it Empurias (after the Greek *emporion,* or trading post).

The Roman city thrived until the 5rd century when Visigothic invasions from the 31

north brought about a rapid decline. By the time the Moors were sweeping through Spain, it stood in ruins, and the sand and silt of centuries had linked San Martín to the mainland.

When La Escala began to expand in the 1600s, the former splendour of Ampurias was only a legend of old, passed down from generation to generation—and a quarry from which the people of La Escala could take stone to build their houses. Great blocks of masonry left for destinations as far afield as Rosas and Perpignan in France.

Then, in 1908, excavations unearthed the boundaries of the 700-by-500-yard ancient settlement of Ampurias and revealed the long-buried treasures of the town. The most sensational find was a larger-than-life statue of Asclepius (the Greek god of medicine), sculpted in marble from an Athenian quarry. The original has been moved to the Barcelona Archaeological Museum, but a copy stands in its place in the ruined temple dedicated to the god. Another copy is in the museum right on the site, which exhibits most of the finds made here.

Wander through the ancient cities of two civilizations; it is a vivid experience. You pass water storage cisterns, ground plans of two patrician villas, huge defence walls, ruined temples, the old market-places, the baths and houses. You'll be able to imagine the place alive with people going about their everyday occupations; you'll marvel at the achievements of their civilization.

Then look in at the museum with its ceramics, jewels, household items, weapons, multicoloured mosaics and statues rescued from centuries of oblivion. Outside the museum, still intact on the mosaic floor, is a touching inscription in Greek that has survived the ravages of time and invasion: "Sweet Dreams".

Ruins of Ampurias bear mute witness to a history of two civilizations.

Estartit

Estartit, at the top of the long Bay of Pals, was only a huddle of modest fishermen's houses at the foot of the striking Roca Maura until the tourist boom of the 1960s transformed it overnight into a thriving holiday spot and a major yachting centre. The broad sandy beach is excellent for children, but beware of the occasional day when waves can be tall. Attractions include launch excursions to coastal destinations inaccessible by land and to the MEDAS ISLANDS, whose jagged profile looms offshore.

The largest island is Meda Gran; you won't find buried treasures here, but at least after a visit to the island, you can claim to have explored a genuine pirates' lair, for Normans, Algerians and Turks all used the islands as a base from which to terrorize the coast. In the 15th century, monks established a fortified monastery there, and during the Peninsular War, the British occupied the territory until driven out by French shore batteries in Estartit. Since 1890, except for the lighthouse, the islands have been uninhabited—to the delight of botanists, who can find over 150 identified species of plants. Five kilometres inland from Estartit lies TORROELLA DE MONTGRÍ, a favourite shopping centre for visitors up and down the coast. Its colourful market sells the pick of local Mediterranean fruit and seafood and some imaginative items from wickerwork artisans of the area.

In the 13th century Torroella was a port, but during the last 700 years, the River Ter has poured so much silt into the

area that the town now lies totally inland. On a barren hill behind stands the gaunt unfinished Montgrí Castle, started on the orders of Jaime II in the 13th century. At that time, Torroella was famous for more than its weavers; it was a renowned cultural and social centre as well. But a 14th-century epidemic decimated the population, and by the 1600s a combination of wars and pirate raids had wrecked the town. The castle serves as a powerful reminder of a time when Torroella was one of the favourite royal hunting retreats.

Left: *Picking from among the many Mediterranean vegetables is a joy.*
Below: *The broad and sandy beaches typify Estartit, a yachting centre.*

Bagur

The next point of importance down the coast is Bagur. In spite of Bagur's location, 4 kilometres inland, the role of the sea can always be felt in the town. Bagur plays "capital" to five small, charming and popular beach resorts strung along the rugged coastline, all quite different in character. First to come, and just out of sight of the long sandy beach of Pals, is SA RIERA, where fishermen's houses mingle with more modern constructions in a successful blend. Then follow AIGUA-FREDA, SA TUNA, FORNELLS and AIGUABLAVA with its mysterious rock formations.

Villas huddle among the trees at Bagur, many belonging to wealthy families from Barcelona, others built by *indianos,* those who returned rich from the Latin-American colonies. These elegant, small mansions, with wrought-iron window grills, arcaded balconies and plain, stark colours on the walls, are surrounded by palm-trees redolent of the tropics. Some of these *indianos* also built similarly attractive summer houses on the beach of Sa Tuna.

The massive ruined castle above Bagur stands on the site of an earlier fortress which withstood countless attacks by Norman and Scandinavian raiders and a motley bunch of Mediterranean pirates. From its ruins you have a magnificent view over the coast and the hinterland.

At Aiguablava, a state-run inn of the national *parador* chain (see below) perches high

Idyllic coves abound in Bagur area.

above a sheltered cove, its foundations built into the rock.

From here, take a boat to the CUEVA D'EN GISPERT, a cave that cuts 900 feet into the cliff. It may take a bit of stiff negotiation with the local fishermen, but the 1–2-hour cruise is well worth-while. And if you don't find Aiguablava's water particularly refreshing, try the nearby Cove of Aigua Gélida ("freezing water"); the difference is astounding.

Spain's Parador Chain

There are nearly one hundred *paradores* (state-run tourist inns) in Spain's national *parador* chain. They are dotted strategically around the country so that a traveller is never more than a day's drive away from one.

Twenty hotels have been installed in converted castles or palaces; a further ten in other buildings of outstanding historical and architectural interest. And apart from elegant surroundings and menus featuring typical regional dishes, *paradores* offer service and facilities unheard of elsewhere in Europe at the price. The organization employs 3,700 people—nearly one staff member per guest (maximum stay: 10 days).

Paradores are not in competition with commercial hotels, and in fact they lose money. Their job is to promote Spain and help open up little-frequented but worthy tourist areas.

The most popular inns are often fully booked two months in advance, so it is advisable to reserve early. On the Costa Brava, there is a very luxurious *parador* at Aiguablava; elsewhere in Catalonia they are located at Vich, Cardona (near a unique salt mountain), Balaguer and Tortosa.

Inland from Bagur

Within easy reach of Bagur are a series of points of interest in the heart of the Catalonian countryside.

Apart from the occasional tractor and roadside advertisement, PALS (5 kilometres from Bagur), in common with a number of other villages in this area, seems barely changed since its origins in the 10th century. Cars can go only as far as the old church; the rest must be visited on foot. The **37** harmonious colour of the stone, the long, walled precincts, the tower *(Torre de las Horas)* crowning the hill, the narrow streets and attractive houses in the process of restoration go to make up a complete living museum.

The charming inland village of Pals, dating from the 10th century, is dominated by Torre de las Horas.

Along with parts of Valencia, further south, the Pals region is one of Spain's rice-growing areas, though this activity is losing its impetus here as time goes by and tourism takes over the key role. Each June, however, the farmers work 12 hours a day up to their knees in the muddy paddies sowing the new crop.

Pals boasts its own beach, PLAYA DE PALS, 6 kilometres

away. Though the tall radio transmitters in the background scarcely contribute to creating a holiday atmosphere, the long stretch of perfect sand —so hot at times it's hard to walk on barefoot—and a golf course spreading out among the pine trees that grow in profusion explain the beach's growing popularity.

Peratallada nestles in the fertile Ampurdán plain, unchanging and unchanged for generations. Once heavily fortified, remnants of its defensive walls still stand, totally integrated into a beautiful stone town of a harmonious grey-yellow hue. Poplars and flowers abound to add touches of colour and life. Old dogs bask in the leaden sun; chickens, flapping their wings hysterically, flutter across beaten-earth tracks (none of the roads are paved); walls, churches, towers, arcades and galleries fit in together in this timeless, most unselfconscious complex. One rather run-down shop and a lonely restaurant bravely represent commercial activity. The names of former owners appear engraved on the lintels of various old houses.

Thirty years ago, ULLESTRET (10 kilometres from Torroella) was an unknown hamlet, charming but unremarkable in the area. Today, the name is familiar to scholars throughout Catalonia and far beyond, for, in 1946, archaeologists excavating the hill of San Andrés unearthed an entire 4th–5th century B.C. **Iberian city.** Lengthy walls have been excavated, grain silos and subterranean water tanks survive, and the whole site has been neatly labeled with plans and numerous explanations. The museum, set amid gardens with benches and even a picnic area, exhibits objects found during the dig. Greek vases stand beside skulls with rusty swords still protruding from them. Arms, instruments, implements, pottery and everyday objects all constitute a small but instructive museum.

Palafrugell

TAMARIÚ, LLAFRANCH and CALELLA (near Cabo Roig Botanical Gardens, with the rocky FORMIGUES ISLANDS offshore) are three deservedly popular and secluded resorts fanning out from inland Palafrugell; each is built on steep hills enclosing picturesque small bays. Pine trees descend right down to sea level, adding their fragrance to the smell of the sea. **39**

Palafrugell, an important market town for the surrounding farming communities, is also a favourite shopping spot for holiday-makers. Unlike Bagur, an inland sea-town, Palafrugell, in spite of its tentacular hold on its resorts, turns its back on the sea to look inland. Its prosperity stems from both a cosmopolitan tourist trade and the cork industry, for it stands on the edge of La Selva, one of the great cork-producing areas of Spain. If, at some point, you feel the need for solitude, you can be alone here with scarcely a sign of human presence, while the coast is no more than 15 kilometres away.

Visit the 15th-century Gothic **Iglesia de San Martín** (Church of St. Martin), restored after Civil War damage. Take a break from shopping to sample a *vino negro* ("black wine") in one of the town's bars. Red wine is called *tinto* elsewhere in Spain, but the dark-red, strong Ampurdán type, with up to 17 per cent alcohol content, deserves its name.

At LA BISBAL (13 kilometres from Palafrugell) further shopping possibilities await a visitor, especially in the way of local pottery—vivid, though not garish. And visit the 13th-century fortified **Palacio de los Obispos** (Palace of the Bishops), now in a poor state of repair. From 844 to 1446, the town was ruled by the Church after it was given to the Bishop of Gerona by the Frankish king, Charles the Bald.

Round La Bisbal lie many other charming villages, such as CRUILLES, MADREMAÑA and MARTIVELL, perfect in their way, totally closed to the industrial world, doomed to decline as their young are irresistibly drawn to the cities.

Palamós

Back now to the coast, with one of the star resorts of the Costa Brava. Palamós's affluence has always been linked with its **port.** In 1299, the Catalonian fleet set out from here to conquer Sicily; the valiant expedition that beat the Turks at Lepanto assembled at Palamós where, on a number of occasions, the French navy also landed its invading forces. Today it harbours the town's sizeable fishing fleet. Alongside, a marina for 500 pleasure and sports-craft symbolizes the community's entry into the tourist industry.

Palamós's fleet casts off at dawn and returns in the late afternoon. The catch, an eye-opening selection of Mediterranean sea-life, provides the ingredients for such delicious Catalan dishes as *suquet de peix*. Watch it being auctioned at 5 o'clock in *La Lonja*, the auction-room. Here is the chance to spend half an hour in the fisherman's world, amongst sea-going boats, wives mending mounds of nets and brawny, rough-talking sea-dogs. No hope of understanding much of what the auctioneer is saying. He mumbles at the rate of 500 words a minute—in Catalan.

Also visit the 15th-century **Church of Santa María del Mar** (St. Mary of the Sea), which still dominates the skyline. During the Spanish Civil War,

Enter the universe of the fisherman at 5 p.m. in Palamós, as the catch of the day is auctioned off briskly.

Palamós was bombed but the church came out unscathed. Damage to the town was repaired by the government's Devastated Regions Service, an organization Palamós could have done with in 1543 when it was sacked by the feared pirate Barbarossa (Red Beard), who meted out the same treatment to Cadaqués. And don't miss the town's **Museo municipal** (Municipal Museum), a dusty, old-fashioned room with exhibits recalling the former thriving cork industry. You'll be overwhelmed by the nuances and qualities there can be of a simple bottle-stopper! Also excellent collections of seashells and coins (Palamós minted its own in the 15th century).

Smooth beach and calm sea combine agreeably for bathers and boaters.

The Southern Stretch

The broad sweep of clean, white beach made Palamós, neighbouring SAN ANTONIO DE CALONGE and PLAYA DE ARO obvious targets for developers. Tourism in fact created Playa de Aro. It is now a pleasant, bustling resort, well planned if one can ignore the towering skyscrapers right on the beach. Some 25 years ago, there existed only the broad, uninterrupted expanse of beach—the rest was open countryside.

S'Agaró and San Feliú de Guixols

Visitors have only words of praise for what they find at S'Agaró (3 kilometres beyond Playa de Aro), small, exclusive and elegant—no untidy *urbanizaciones* or haphazard planning here.

The town, begun from scratch in 1923, was the brainchild of a Barcelona businessman, José Ensesa, who set out to transform a few empty acres into a residential town without ugly urban sprawl. He set up iron-clad contracts with his clients to guarantee the architectural integrity of the project and took advantage of the rocky cliffs (for we have again left behind the long, sandy stretches). All the luxurious houses cling to seaside cliffs or peer discreetly through deep pine-tree cover. There are parks, public and private gardens, lookout points, rotundas and the magnificent 2½-mile-long promenade, the **Camino de Ronda,** a promenade that follows the contour of the coast. Steps lead down to LA CONÇA beach on one side of the town, while SAN POL beach on the other is the only place on the Costa Brava where there is a small charge to go onto the sand and make use of the bathing huts.

In keeping with this aura of exclusivity, S'Agaró boasts one of Spain's most famous hotels, the Hostal de La Gavina, where you will have no trouble whatsoever spending a small fortune for an—admittedly—unforgettable stay, perhaps in the Louis XV suite with marble bathroom and genuine period furniture, or, more modestly, in a double room where your slightest wish is a command.

According to tradition, the Iberian King Brigo, searching for an easily defensible yet beautiful bay, fell for the site of San Feliú de Guixols and had a castle built there, captured centuries later by **43**

the Moors. Later still, Charlemagne converted it into a Benedictine monastery which still exists, though changed and restored over the years. Today, remnants of the original survive amidst some Gothic architecture, such as the **Porta Ferrada,** an elegant, arcaded 11th-century gallery, restored in 1931, and the **Torre del Fum** (Smoke Signal Tower) where fires were lit to warn of pirate attack. The museum, close by, in its modest way, confirms the breadth of the town's history.

San Feliú, the self-dubbed "Queen of the Costa Brava", lies 3 kilometres south of S'Agaró and shares the beach (the non-exclusive part) with it. Bright and pleasant, with a large resident population, San Feliú has just about everything that can be expected of a Costa Brava holiday. This long-established resort exudes a stylish Riviera-like charm and has avoided the look of a boom town. At the same time, it provides all the necessary amenities—good shops and restaurants, tours and excursions by land or sea, a yacht marina, golf club, tennis courts, riding stables, nightclubs and a bullring. It has a short but active promenade, its Ramblas, and an exceptionally broad and beautiful marine boulevard. The elegant old buildings lining this leafy **Paseo del Mar** were designed as casinos (but betting in this form was banned in 1924). The beach in front is broad, sandy and open, with the possibility of trips up to more deserted coves and crags, difficult of access except by boat. For the best view of the town and typical coastal scenery it is worth taking a short walk to the **Ermita de Sant Elm** (Hermitage of St. Elm). From here, the town looks neat and prosperous (its original wealth came essentially from the cork industry); turn to face the south and the rugged coast stretches away towards Tossa, 22 kilometres beyond. The churning sea below surges around the rocks, sucking the waters into crannies and spewing them out furiously. A plaque cut into the rock mentions that on this spot, Ferrán Agulló conceived the idea of baptizing the coast Costa Brava ("wild coast").

Night-time activity now concentrates on bars, clubs and discotheques, and on the *Paseo* itself, where, on warm nights, families and courting couples stroll and chat in the inimitable Iberian babble of excitement and communication. Once a week in the summer (check at the Tourist Office right behind the Paseo del Mar), the *sardana* is danced on the *Paseo*. If you feel the urge, join in with a fringe group (see p. 81). But don't be upset if you find yourself edged out for upsetting the tempo of the entire circle.

Inland from San Feliú

On a hilltop 6 kilometres from San Feliú is Pedralta, Iberia's biggest balancing rock. One huge stone atop another of the same caliber can be levered and rocked without it toppling. To get there, leave San Feliú on the Gerona road, and at the last row of houses in the town, take the small turning to the left. But if you drive, don't be too hard on your car's suspension, as the track becomes progressively more bumpy and full of potholes.

CALDAS DE MALAVELLA (23 kilometres inland from San Feliú) can claim no prominent sons and was never the scene of a famous battle; yet it has enjoyed a widespread reputation for 2,000 years. *Calda* means a hot mineral water spring, and the spas at Caldas have been visited since Roman times by sufferers from gastric **45** and rheumatic complaints. In 1883, the water was declared "of public utility" and now it is bottled commercially. But you can drink it as it emerges from the ground—only beware: it's so hot it almost scorches your mouth. It dribbles pitifully from a small fountain behind the Roman remains. You'll notice a few bottles lying beside the rather insignificant fountain waiting to be picked up. Another, and somewhat more grandiose, fountain at the entrance to the town gushes forth torrents when operated manually.

Driving up the N11 near SILS, at kilometre 706, you will find the **Colección de Automóviles de Salvador Claret** (the Salvador Claret Vintage Car Museum). Señor Claret started his collection 50 years ago and now has a display of 80 antique cars, each reconditioned by him personally and each in perfect working order. The oldest is an 1883 single-cylinder, coal-burning Merry Weather.

♂ Tossa de Mar

From San Feliú to Tossa (a distance of 22 kilometres), the road twists and turns, following the sinuous course of the coast. Few of the hidden creeks are easily accessible, but the views are magnificent. Keep an eye on the road.

Of all the big resorts on the Costa Brava, Tossa de Mar can claim to be one of the most attractive.

Twenty years before Spain's tourist boom got under way, Tossa was a hideaway for artists in search of cheap living, beautiful surroundings and mild weather. Things have not greatly changed: then, as now, Spain was relatively cheap and the Mediterranean summer meant dazzling sunrise and endless dusk. The white village with a touch of the South and the profile of the old fortified city standing out against the southern skyline, spelled paradise for painters and writers sick of the grit and grime of city life.

No Tossa School as such emerged, but fine work was produced in this fishing village clustered harmoniously round Tossa Bay. Roads of the old town are named after the main Catalan artists such as the Plaza del pintor J. Villalonga, and examples of their work hang today in the museum built right into the walls of Vila Vella (the old fortified city)—gifts from those artists who at one time or another called Tossa home.

The museum also displays

relics of Tossa's Roman era, when it was known as Turissa. At the back of the town, on its outskirts, you can see an excavated Roman villa, complete with mosaics, its own swimming pool and a sophisticated heating system. Children, under careful surveillance, excavate further with all the enthusiasm of gold-diggers.

The great 12th-century walls of **Vila Vella** (3 feet thick in places and some 23 feet high) once held back savage marauders. By the 17th century, the town had started to outgrow its walls; a new church was consecrated in 1776 just in front of the large beach round the bay, and around it sprang up the modern town. Delightful, fresh

Tossa's ramparts form backdrop for bathers as new houses gleam in sun.

and inviting though this new town is, visitors tend to head to Vila Vella to inspect its crumbling archways, rough cobbled streets with a profusion of flowers and a galaxy of galleries, bars and restaurants in ancient houses built of the same stone as the ramparts. Remains of medieval wall house tool sheds and dog kennels.

The fortified wall encircles the hill on which the old town lies; one tower *(Torre Major)* and part of the wall that gave onto the sea were demolished to make way for the lighthouse, but three towers remain, and a magnificent view can be had of "wild" coastal scenery.

There is something of an air of conspiracy, of smuggling and piracy about the minute **Es Codolar Cove,** tucked away at the back of Vila Vella and enclosed on either side by abrupt hillsides. In fact, however, this cove has for centuries provided safe anchorage for Tossa's fishermen and was their original home. Their boats are pulled high up the slope of the beach almost to the foot of the last tower. The slowly diminishing number of fishermen share the cove with tourists who swim there during the day, sometimes turning up early in the morning to watch the catch brought home.

The rocky coast between here and Blanes, 20 kilometres further down the coast, is much appreciated by skin-divers.

Only a narrow riverbed, dry most of the year and crossed by a modest wooden bridge, separates modern Tossa from its main beach. Down on the sand, booths sell excursion tickets for boats bobbing in the shallows. Even when dusk approaches, "action" scarcely moves from the water's edge. Beachside restaurants spring to life as hundreds of hungry holiday-makers pack outdoor tables and unhurriedly sip aperitifs as they wait to eat at the Spanish hour—when the heat of the day has abated. And, just before darkness falls, arc lamps silently explode into life, throwing into relief the venerable walls of Vila Vella against an ink-blue sky.

Lloret de Mar

There could scarcely be a bigger contrast to Tossa than Lloret de Mar: the one town is slow-moving, leisurely; the other, brash, full of life, noise, movement.

Lloret is unabashedly, enthusiastically a tourist town—with a Spanish coloration. It hasn't the beauty of Tossa, but, for animated nightlife, for "holiday life" in community, there is no town on the Costa Brava like Lloret. More than 200 hotels, one casino, and shops, discos, clubs and restaurants by the thousand are jumbled behind the palm-shaded **Paseo Verdaguer.** This boulevard, perhaps the most elegant seafront promenade on the entire Costa Brava, provides a fine background for the immense, broad sandy beach sweeping around Lloret Bay.

On a rocky promontory at one end of the bay stands a mighty, turreted castle whose medieval outline is an obvious favourite with photographers. But on closer inspection, if you feel something amiss, something a bit too perfect, you would be right: the castle (a classic postcard view) is Lloret's very own folly, built this century by a Barcelona businessman who had the bank-balance to match his dreams.

The maze of streets leading into the Paseo Verdaguer form the heart of a cosmopolitan shopping centre—don't even attempt to enter by car. To get the feel of Lloret's multinational character, just take a stroll round in early evening. Here, amid a wild contrast of exotic aromas and multilingual neon signs, German beerhalls compete with English tearooms and the fish-and-chips shops; here, smørgåsbord, spaghetti, sauerkraut, sausages, mash and other "imported" dishes are in heavy demand by sun-tanned hordes,

Barcelona businessman built castle "guarding" beach at Lloret de Mar.

ravenous after their daily beach stints. Search hard enough amongst the crowded streets and culinary hotch- **49** potch and you'll even find Catalan and Spanish specialities—in a restaurant most likely owned by a Finn or an Englishman.

Lloret today has no industry but tourism, yet its history and traditions go back centuries. Probably founded by the Iberians, it was certainly colonized by the Romans. In the Middle Ages, it boasted a serious castle, and, in the 13th century, Italian sailors formed a colony here.

The ship-building industry has disappeared now, and the fishing fleet has dwindled to a handful of boats beached in La Caleta Cove. Tourism has swept all before it: fishermen have become shop-owners and bartenders; farmers, property magnates; brick-layers, contractors and promotors. One fisherman whose great-great-grandfather died in South American swamps searching for gold found *his* gold-mine without leaving home. His family's sea-side shanty became valuable overnight and is now the site of a ten-storey, three-star hotel.

A few calm islets held out, however, against the invasion. One or two dour fishermen tend their nets stoically; Tuesday remains market-day; on Sunday, black-shrouded wom-en hurry arm in arm past bikini-clad visitors to attend mass at **San Román,** Lloret's 16th-century church with its multi-coloured tiles standing out like a sore thumb. And almost any balmy evening, groups of villagers may gather to dance the *sardana* beneath the palms of Pasco Verdaguer, which maintains its dignified old-world charm. The best way to take in Lloret's possibilities is to stand and admire the graceful curve of the lovely bay from here.

Lloret's most popular annual fiesta, enjoyed equally by townspeople and tourists, is held in honour of St. Christine, an Italian martyr killed by arrows. Her corpse was hurled into the sea with a stone attached and found still intact by Lloret fishermen months later. A **hermitage** was built in St. Christine's honour on the pine-covered bluff above the beach where her body was found. The delightful beach, with its single hotel and cultivated fields all round, was named after her and she was also made Lloret's Protector of Fishermen.

Now, each year, on the morning of July 24th, decorated boats are launched from Lloret to sail the nearly 2 miles to **Santa Cristina Cove.** Then, boatmen and ex-boatmen, returning to their original profession for the day, and hundreds of lazier villagers who have travelled by road, climb to the hermitage to pay homage to the saint—and celebrate afterwards in the hearty Catalan way.

Costa Brava lures the adventurous.

Blanes

For Blanes, tourism is just a rich bonus for an already stable economy. Its deep-sea fishing fleet remains in action, farmers continue to till the surrounding land, and a booming nylon factory employs 4,000 workers. Blanes's long history has left noteworthy ruins and its beaches are as fine as any on the Catalonian coast. A long maritime promenade, with

playground and carpark, faces a beach with two minute islands which mark the official limit of the Costa Brava.

Hints of Blanes's past wealth can be seen on the seafront: some of the aristocratic houses, mingling in with the modern blocks, were built by *indianos* back from Latin America.

Behind the seafront, the town has kept its character of a fishing town (though this industry has become secondary) with a maze of narrow backstreets. The names are in Spanish—and in Catalan.

The wild beauty of the cliffs along its northern shoreline has attracted a large number of nature-lovers to make their home in Blanes. One of the first was Carlos Faust, born in Germany in 1874, who emigrated to Spain in his youth. After making his fortune in

These rugged fishermen, busily at work on their trawler, perpetuate the sea-going tradition in Blanes.

Barcelona, he came to Blanes and bought a large plot of land north of the town overlooking the Mediterranean. There, in 1928, he planted a garden, **Marimurtra** (sea and myrtle), which gained fame throughout the botanical world. He had arranged for the gardens to pass to a trust after his death in 1952, and now Marimurtra is tended by botanists and a team of nine gardeners who look after more than 3,000 different species of trees, shrubs and flowers. From the rotunda on a rocky promontory at the edge of the gardens, you see a Capuchin monastery plus some breathtaking seascapes. Open to the public, Marimurtra is a major attraction; the serene beauty and the dazzling colours of the flowers make a welcome change from the beach.

On the quay in Blanes, two glimpses of the world of the deep: first, at the **aquarium,** with its living panorama of Mediterranean sea life; then, at the daily fish auction (held nearby), with more of the same... but ready for filleting.

In town, look in on the **Parish Church of Santa María** (St. Mary's). Built in the 14th century, it was restored after serious damage in the Civil War, though the outside has retained all its charm. Inside, the vault keystones carry the coats-of-arms of the Cabrera family, who owned whole tracts of countryside throughout Catalonia. Their palace once was linked to the church. Today a few bits of rubble testify to the building's existence; also, some 300 yards beyond, half hidden down one of the main streets, is a 15th-century Gothic fountain which served the household.

Blanes is the southernmost coastal town in the Province of Gerona; we have come to the end of the Costa Brava. The coastline changes character, losing its "wild" look to

become flat, with long sandy beaches and the *Maresme.* South of Blanes begins the Costa Dorada.* Inland from Blanes and on the border with Barcelona Province stands the intriguing 11th-century walled village of HOSTALRICH.

The renowned Marimurtra Gardens in Blanes, laid out in 1928, attract both the botanist and the tourist.

---

* See the Berlitz COSTA DORADA AND BARCELONA TRAVEL GUIDE.

✿ Gerona—Capital of the Costa Brava

Bridges and staircases—this is the image you are likely to take back with you of Gerona. You will be surprised by the fascination of this small city of 50,000 people. Turn almost any corner in old Gerona and you'll come upon some surprising monument, a revelation or a delight. Stairways worn smooth by centuries of footsteps lead under arches invaded by weeds. Narrow alleys, cobbled tracks between crumbling walls, guide you through a medieval panorama.

Capital of the province and, by extension, of the Costa Brava, Gerona lies just 35 kilometres from San Feliú de Guixols, the closest resort, and less than 80 from Port Bou, the furthest. A trip to this compact town with a long history is an ideal opportunity to sample Spanish city life and at the same time a chance to shop at competitive prices. From anywhere on the Costa Brava, the journey and some leisurely sightseeing can be fitted comfortably into one day.

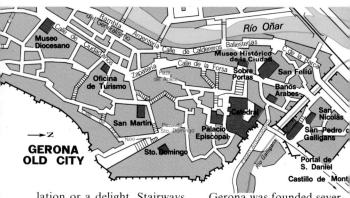

Gerona was founded several centuries B.C. at the confluence of the Rivers Ter and Oñar. Ten bridges (some for pedestrians only) and an entire square cross the Oñar as it cuts through the town. Although the river normally runs 10 feet below tenements and shops whose windows hang out romantically over the waters, it has, more prosaically, been a source of misery since time immemorial to the Geronese; the river quite regularly overflows—eight or ten times a century since records began in the 13th century. One bar, so close to the river as to be uninsurable, has wall marks recording the heights of no less than six floods, one as recently as 1970.

The River Oñar divides the city neatly in two, a geographical convenience helping visitors find their bearings. In front is the old quarter, called **Barrio de la Catedral,** containing all that is of interest to the visitor, and behind, Barrio del Mercadal, the far bigger commercial and residential section.

The most typical street of the old part is the steep and narrow **Calle de la Forsa,** once the heart of the old Jewish quarter. Art galleries, antique shops, printing shops and stalls specializing in precious books blend discreetly with the stern Gothic architecture of its ancient buildings. At No. 13 is the **Museo Histórico de la Ciudad** (Museum of City History), with exhibits recalling notable Geronese feats of arms and an entire room devoted to manuscripts of Geronese *sardana* music.

Strolling up the Calle de la Forsa, you feel that no real upheaval has changed life since the Middle Ages—except for the plague of cars barely able to turn in the tight one-way streets. Don't even attempt to drive up to the cathedral.

Calle de la Forsa runs directly to the Plaza de la Catedral. A fine monumental Baroque stairway of 90 steps leads up to the cathedral's Door of the Apostles, a magnificent entrance so badly damaged during the Civil War that only two of the 12 apostles' statues are originals. The **cathedral** dates from the 11th century, but was subsequently enlarged during the 14th and 15th. The result is a nave of impressive proportions, flanked all round by 30 side chapels. If light and your eyes permit, try to scrutinize the vault keystones of these chapels. Each is a masterpiece in itself.

Through huge stained-glass windows, the muted light filters onto the gilded altarpieces of the chapels and illuminates the majestic interior, usually empty of chairs; rarely does a cathedral present such an awesome sight. The carved, alabaster high altar has served the church since its consecration day in 1038. In the adjoining **55** chapter-house, the **cathedral treasure** includes two important items: in a room to itself, a 12th-century tapestry in charming low-key colours telling the story of the Creation, and the *Book of the Apocalypse,* an illuminated manuscript of texts and commentaries compiled by a certain Friar Beato in the Asturian Monastery of Liébana in A.D. 975. There are also superb

medieval gold and silver plates, magnificent medieval Catalonian wooden sculptures and paintings, and some lovely Moorish chests.

In a region where beautiful cloisters are relatively abundant, Gerona's **cloister** is exceptional; the anecdotal Old Testament sculpture will delight you. Two angels sit chatting on a wall. A sheepish, bearded Adam has a bite from an apple resembling a hand grenade. In front of the restful cloister, the 12th-century Romanesque bell tower, called "Charlemagne's Tower", rises imposingly.

Squatting at the cathedral's feet, though a fairly massive work itself, is the **Iglesia de San Feliú** (St. Felix's Church), thought to stand over catacombs where the 4th-century St. Narcissus was martyred during a secret Mass. The catacombs were Gerona's first Christian burial ground. St. Felix, also martyred, was the 4th-century Bishop of Gerona and is now the city's patron saint. The church's foundations were laid in 1313 and the building completed in 1392. The elegant Gothic spire, mimicked by the nearby pop-

Immortal view of Gerona's colourful skyline is reflected in River Oñar.

lars, remains one of Gerona's most delightful and characteristic landmarks, for its top ten feet were lopped off by lightning in 1581 and never replaced. Inside, you'll see Roman (or, in fact, early-Christian) sarcophaguses with beautifully carved scenes of the life of Susanna and Narcissus's own very fine tomb.

Tucked away behind a wall near the cathedral, the so-called **Baños Arabes** (Arab Baths) were built 400 years after the Moors were expelled from Catalonia; they imitate a Moorish style modelled in turn on Roman baths. Visit the graceful octagonal *frigidarium* (cold bath), the *tepidarium* (warm bath) and *caldarium* (steam bath).

Gerona's fairly modest **Museo Arqueológico** (Ar-

chaeological Museum) is a building of exceptional beauty—the former 12th-century Benedictine **Monastery of San Pedro de Galligans.** Its exhibits include Greek and Roman objects excavated at Ampurias (see p. 32), paintings, including works by Tintoretto and Murillo, and a rare 17th-century printing press. Each May, culture bows to horticulture, and the cool, arcaded

Regal staircases, bridges, arches form the hallmarks of old Gerona.

monastery cloisters are host to the province's best attended flower display. Note just beside the museum the very delightful Romanesque Church of San Nicolás.

Go up some flights of stairs beyond San Pedro and join the **Paseo Arqueológico** (Archaeological Promenade), meandering along the medieval walls which defended Gerona (sometimes not too successfully) in no fewer than 34 sieges. Walls, ruined or still standing, battlements, old houses, abandoned or otherwise, appear, disappear, reappear over several hundred yards. Massive towers and buttresses resist, testifying to the moments of glory and

Gerona façades—a colour quilt.

decline of a city strategically built to control the plain—and thus the road south—between the Pyrenees and the sea.

The most unusual, profitable and picturesque shopping is to be had in the old quarter. Centuries-old shops with painted wooden fronts remind a visitor that in Gerona shopping remains a community affair, not a mad in-and-out rush to grab a few ready-packaged necessities. Here in the casual muddle of Geronese alleys, family businesses flourish. Grocers display tasty, locally produced sausage and cheese, and scoop cereals from open vats or olives galore from great containers. Little old ladies, "embroidery specialists", hand-sew initials onto linen; the owner of a *corsetería,* or corset shop, will happily make garments to fit anyone's particular problem.

The shaded Rambla del Generalísimo, running parallel to the River Oñar, fills the need of every Spanish town for an elegant meeting place. In the mornings, it blazes with colour as flower-sellers bustle amid their dazzling displays. Late afternoon, friends of all states and ages come together for aperitifs and gossip. With the evening appear the *sardana* dancers and the young who wander endlessly arm-in-arm back and forth along its length, chatting noisily over the general hubbub.

At sunset, people stroll past the Ramblas and lean on the railings to stare at the river.

The Road to Andorra

The road to Andorra, after leaving the coast and passing through Gerona, begins to rise to the Pyrenees. It follows essentially the same route as the so-called Romanesque Road, which is studded with numerous architectural gems of this period.

While Romanesque art in other Spanish provinces shows distinct Arab influences, in Catalonia, there are more traces of Lombard and Frankish art. The Geronese route links up with the *Route Romane du Roussillon* on the French side of the Pyrenees; Roussillon was part of the Catalonian-Aragonese kingdom until the Treaty of the Pyrenees in 1659, when it was handed over to France.

Bañolas

Bañolas, 18 kilometres from Gerona, is a rarity in Spain; a town with a lake. Its origins go back to the Visigothic period and relics of its long history are to be found scattered round the town: a 13th-century church, a monastery dating

A Spanish rarity: Bañolas, a town which boasts a lake of its own.

back to the 9th century and the **Plaza de España,** bordered all round by an arcade and 15th-century houses. The **Museo Arqueológico** (Archaeological Museum), installed in a carefully restored 15th-century house, boasts Roman and medieval exhibits and the city's historical archives.

The **lake** is a peaceful picnic spot, with cafés purveying food and drink, couples lazily

rowing in search of quiet spots amongst tall trees lining the shore and artists seeking to capture pastel shades on their canvas. Bañolas has also become an important centre for fishing, sailing and water-skiing competitions.

On the opposite side of the lake from Bañolas lies **Porqueras,** a hamlet of two houses, whose small, exquisite 12th-century Romanesque church between the row of trees is a perfect example of harmony between architecture and nature.

Besalú

Besalú captures the spirit of medieval Catalonia at the height of its power in a way no other town does. It may have been founded by the Celts, was certainly an important Roman stronghold, and reached its zenith between the 9th and 12th centuries, when it was the home of the Counts of Besalú.

Monuments still surviving amongst the narrow stone streets include the thousand-year-old **Iglesia de San Vicente** (St. Vincent's Church), which suffered in the Civil War. When reconstruction started, a vase was found beneath the altar containing gold coins and unidentified religious relics. The **Monasterio de San Pedro** (St. Peter's Monastery), founded in 997, and the evocative ruins of the **Iglesia de Santa María** (St. Mary's Church), dating from 1055, are located in the upper part of town on a site once occupied by a castle and now private land. Besalú's most famed landmark, admired even by those who drive by the town without stopping, is the arched and fortified **medieval bridge,** recently restored and classified as a national monument. As so often in Spain, a fine massive structure crosses a mere trickle of a stream far below.

Between Besalú and Olot, 20 kilometres away, the village of **Castellfullit de la Roca** perches on a dramatic spur of rock over 300 feet above the River Fluviá. Its church at one end and the rows of houses seem to be suspended over the abyss like the prow of some gigantic stranded ship, while away beyond, the terraced fields climb towards open hills. It is a spectacular sight, particularly at night.

Camprodón

Twisting and turning as it rises from Olot, the road to Camprodón, 30 kilometres north, takes us to another world. The **61**

mountain air is brisk and bracing, the shops are overflowing with Pyrenean sausage, cheeses, ham; the people look robust and red-cheeked. At an altitude of over 3,000 feet, and a mere 17 kilometres from the French border, Camprodón is a quite exceptionally pretty mountain village. Have a look before entering the village at the 10th-century **Monastery of San Pedro.**

The town straggles along the confluence of the Rivers Ter and Ritort, forming a perfect *Y*-shape. The focal point is the high-arched 15th-century bridge, inexplicably called **Puente Nuevo,** or the "new bridge". Excellent fishing and shooting and nearby skiing have made the town a favourite with Geronese, who come on regular weekend pilgrimages here.

But the charm of the village is its houses hanging out over the River Ter as it dashes down from the mountains; for the Ter here has none of the sluggish appearance it does in Gerona most of the year round.

Ripoll

The comfortable road descending from Camprodón to Ripoll (some 24 kilometres)

follows the timeless route taken by pilgrims and travellers from France. On the way, stop at the delightful village of **San Pablo de Seguríes** and at the **Monastery of San Juan de las Abadesas** (St. John of the Nuns). The fine light sculpture of the cloisters, betraying a French influence, contrasts with the massive effect of the interior. Note, too, the **Sant Misteri,** a remarkable sculptural group dating from 1250, full of life and movement.

The **Monasterio de Santa María de Ripoll** (Monastery of St. Mary of Ripoll) is the Westminster Abbey of Catalonia, the key to the Romanesque Road, and the depository (with Montserrat) of the Catalan soul, its history and aspirations. Inside the church rest the bodies of Wifredo el Velloso (Wilfred the Hairy), Count of Barcelona and first ruler of an independent Catalonia; Berenguer III, who expanded the Catalan kingdom and built its navy; and Berenguer IV, the saint, who drove the Moors from their last toehold in his empire. Part of the church is being dug up to reveal even earlier foundations.

Begun in 879 on the orders of Wifredo el Velloso, the monastery, which served as a cementing factor for all Catalans, found itself in a strategic position on the cusp of Europe and Iberia and grew in importance as an exchange floor for ideas and learning between the two cultures. The decline of the Counts of Barcelona heralded its own decline for long centuries.

By 1835, the Monastery of Santa María had fallen into ruin. Only through the zeal and efforts of a certain Bishop Morgades, who took it in hand, was the building saved from complete devastation. Before the century's end, the weary prelate could contemplate the finished work and the monastery was reconsecrated.

Nothing at the monastery quite equals the magnificent 12th-century arched **doorway** leading into the church, described as "the Bible in stone" and "the triumphal Arch of Catholicism". More than 200 carved stone figures in seven horizontal bands tell the story of the Old and New Testaments. A superb example of genuine folk-art, it was carved to illustrate the Bible in an easily intelligible way to country people, many of them illiterate. To give the story immediacy and impact, each figure is carved wearing contemporary Catalan costume.

Another treasure here is Santa María's two-storeyed Romanesque **cloister,** built between the 12th and 14th centuries. The trapezoidal garden is surrounded by 252 columns (126 on each level), each with intricately carved capitals supporting 55 graceful arches.

Resplendent arched doorway graces Monastery of St. Mary of Ripoll.

The shafts of the older columns were fashioned from reddish jasper.

Right beside the monastery is the **Museo de Arte Pirenaico** (Museum of Pyrenean Art). A pleasurable surprise—a spiral staircase winds up a tower to give access to a truly excellent, medium-sized collection, beautifully laid out, of toys, clothes, all sorts of household implements, rural worktools,

Andorra

Nobody can claim to have seen the world without a stop in Andorra, the Biggest Small Country in Europe (its own boast), a 187-square-mile political anachronism.

The principality huddles between mountain peaks in the Pyrenees, surrounded by Spain and France. Of a population of 26,000, a mere 7,926

The change from warm, sea breezes to brisk, mountain air is felt at Camprodón, in its Pyrenean setting.

ceramics and textiles, which provides a vivid general impression of Catalonian country life over the last two centuries.

are Andorrans born and bred. The rest are immigrants attracted by the mountain air and...the income tax system. It's non-existent.

Nor is there a customs service. The shopping is a dream. After 700 years of fiercely defended independence, the country's spectacular scenery now takes second place; most of today's visitors are heading straight for the tax-free cameras, hi-fis and whisky in the bulging shops of Merrinitx Street, in **Andorra La Vella,** the capital. Three million tourists pass through the town every year, mostly with bargains in mind.

Andorra is the only country in which the official language is Catalan. Spanish and French are almost universally understood, while English and German are most useful in the shops. French francs and Spanish pesetas are equally valid in Andorra. In practice, almost any foreign currency is recognized and accepted by the merchants. In smaller shops of Merrinitx Street, bargaining is appropriate. Astute haggling should win a 10 per cent discount.

The country has no armed forces. It successfully escaped involvement in both World Wars and the Spanish Civil War. Though there is a 24-man police force, there's no jail. Crime is rare—unless you count a bit of smuggling as a mortal sin. The main job of the police force is slowing down the 10,000 duty-free Andorran cars zooming round the highways. Significantly, the state picks up a lot of revenue from traffic fines.

Since 1278, Andorra has been under the joint suzerainty of the Spanish bishop of nearby Urgel and the French Counts of Foix (now represented by the President of France). A feudal tithe still must be paid. In alternate years, the French President receives 900 francs, and the bishop collects 450 pesetas, six hams, 12 chickens and 24 cheeses.

Andorra leans heavily on tourism for its income, yet there's no airport or rail system, only roads. Even then, in the whole country there are more miles of trout streams than paved roads. Hunters enjoy nearly 80 square miles of game reserves, all alive with rabbit, hare, partridge and chamois. Some fine skiing is to be had at Grau Roig, Soldeu and Arinsal. There are curative springs in Les Escaldes. And everywhere, peace and quiet.

Utopia? What other country would spend 250,000 pesetas for one rip-roaring fiesta, while appropriating a defence budget of only 300 pesetas?

Barcelona

The chances are your trip to Barcelona will only be a side trip or excursion from the Costa Brava.* Your time will then be limited and so the best idea is to make a tour of the compact old part of the town. If you can prolong your stay in the capital, there is no lack of other areas of interest: the modern city that grew up in the 19th and early 20th centuries, with long, straight and leafy avenues; the portside area, strong on atmosphere and local colour; Montjuich, the mountain to the south of Barcelona with everything from fairgrounds to museums, and reached by aerial cable-car.

The Barrio Gótico
(Gothic Quarter)
The nucleus of old Barcelona, the Barrio Gótico, is concentrated round the cathedral. Here are elements from just about every century since the Iberian tribesmen first settled on the site over 2,000 years ago.

On the spot where the cathedral stands today, the Romans

---

* Tourists settling in for over a day will find a complete guide to Barcelona in another book in this series, the Berlitz COSTA DORADA AND BARCELONA TRAVEL GUIDE.

dedicated a temple to Hercules (you will see three remaining columns in nearby Calle del Paradís). Two early Christian basilicas stood on the same site before the construction of the present **Catedral de Santa Eulalia** between 1298 and 1454. Don't be taken in by that façade, however—it wasn't built until the end of the 19th century, when new work on the cathedral began, thanks to a subsidy from a rich industrialist. Some critics complain that he spoilt the pure Catalan Gothic effect. But don't worry about the critics. Come back, if you can, one night when the delicate spires are illuminated and light glows through the stained-glass windows from the inside. You can scarcely fail to be impressed.

The interior is laid out in classic Catalan Gothic form, with three aisles neatly engineered to produce an effect of grandeur and uplift. Impossibly slender columns soar upwards to support the nave; muted golden light filtering through 500-year-old stained-glass windows adds to the extraordinary effect of spaciousness—one of the most striking characteristics of Catalan Gothic architecture.

Below the altar, go down to the Crypt of St. Eulalia, the 13-

year-old martyr to whom this cathedral is dedicated. Explicit bas-relief carvings on the 14th-century alabaster sarcophagus supply vividly gruesome details of her torture and execution. Behind the altar, at the Chapel of the Holy Sacrament, have a look at the Christ of Lepanto. Juan de Austria carried this sacred image into the decisive sea battle of Lepanto (Spaniards and Venetians versus the Turks), and legend has it that the Christ image moved its body at precisely the right moment to escape a bullet.

At this point, a strange squawking will draw you out into the **cloister**—to be greeted by the sight of a pack of white geese frolicking in a pool of water, surrounded by palm trees, green plants, a fountain and fine, pure Gothic architecture. Generations of their ancestors have also lived here.

Pride of the **Cathedral Museum,** with its religious paintings and sculpture from the 14th century onwards, is undoubtedly the *Piedad del Arcediano Desplá,* executed in 1490 by Bartolomé Bermejo on commission from an egocentric archdeacon, who is pictured kneeling in the foreground of this transcendental biblical scene.

A short walk down Calle de la Tapinería—where cobblers made shoes called *tapín*—leads to Plaza de Berenguer el Grande. Behind the modern equestrian statue of Ramón Berenguer III (who ruled Catalonia from 1096 to 1131) stands a reconstructed Roman wall. You can follow the wall for a fair distance on either side of the Plaza del Angel. Sections of this ancient fortification come to light in incongruous places: "Roman wall visible inside" boasts a notice outside one Gothic Quarter boutique.

In the nearby **Museo de Historia de la Ciudad** (Museum of City History), a converted, stately 16th-century palace, there are paintings, tapestries, maps and documents of municipal import. But the real spectacle is below ground. Beneath this museum are the remains of a settlement the Romans called Julia Faventia Augusta Pia Barcino. You can follow the paths of that civilization around the foundations of the houses, a drainage system, roads, market-places. The well-lit, clearly documented archaeological zone now extends as far afield as the subsoil beneath the cathedral.

The museum windows face

onto **Plaza del Rey** (King's Square), where, in the Middle Ages, farmers sold their produce and locksmiths made bolts. In front, **Salón del Tinell** (Tinell Hall), where Columbus may have been welcomed by Ferdinand and Isabella on his return from America. The extraordinary span of the meeting hall's ceiling, without a column or support, represents a remarkable technical feat.

Beside the hall, the Archives of the Crown of Aragon house documents dating back to the 9th century and some very ancient books. The archives are off-limits to tourists—unless they can lay claim to being scholars.

Two other absolutely major buildings of medieval civic ar-

Rooftops of Barcelona, old and new, viewed from an art-nouveau terrace.

chitecture remain to be visited: the Diputación (Provincial Council) and Ayuntamiento (City Hall), facing one another on Plaza de San Jaime. The **Diputación,** formerly seat of the Catalonian parliament, is interesting not only for its stately architecture, but also the striking details of its decoration (particularly sumptuous in the St. George's Room). You will never be allowed to forget St. George was the patron saint of Catalonia as well as of England, and the same figure is to be found all over the town. Upstairs, too, is a charming orange-tree courtyard.

The **Ayuntamiento** should be seen from Calle de la Ciudad to appreciate the original 14th-century façade. The building still serves, from time to time, for ceremonial meetings and the impressive 14th-century Salón del Consejo de Ciento (Hall of the Council of One Hundred) does honour to any assembly.

La Rambla and the Barrio Chino

La Rambla is a boulevard running east to west, a broad strip of throbbing life over a mile long bordered by two busy arteries. But La Rambla is more: it is an outdoor market, a caldron of gossip, a hotbed of café life, a thieves' den, a lovers' rendezvous. Beneath the linking branches of La Rambla's plane trees, all the different elements of Barcelona fuse.

Symbol of Barcelona's architectural vitality, Church of Sagrada Familia dominates vista of Catalan capital.

Every couple of cross-streets, the Rambla's character changes. So does its official name: Rambla de los Estudios, Rambla de los Capuchinos, Rambla de Santa Mónica and the others—five in all—which explains why very often it's simply referred to as Las Ramblas.

To walk down La Rambla's full extent from the Plaza de Cataluña to the Monumento a Colón (Columbus Monument) is an experience, an entertainment and an education. You can buy a canary, a monkey, a mouse or a turtle; a carnation, an orchid, a potted plant or a bird-of-paradise flower, a packet of nuts or one cigarette from a news-stand. Here the bookstalls stock all the papers and magazines of Europe, gypsies insinuate hot watches, lottery sellers flutter tickets practically guaranteed to win you a million.

Visit the **frontón** to see a game of *pelota* (called *jai-alai* in the Basque country). The ball flashes around the court at speeds of up to 125 miles per hour. The betting around you is even more frantic; split tennis balls stuffed with gaming slips whizz overhead. You can also have your portrait taken by a lady photographer operating a camera so old it has no lens. To expose the film, she snaps a cap in front of the aperture. Or look at a peep-show—mostly of views of Barcelona.

Need a rest? Stop at one of the multitude of bars and cafés lining La Rambla while traffic streams by in a seemingly endless flow, barely noticed—except by the waiters, brandishing their trays aloft, who dodge to and fro to their sources of supply between serried ranks of cars.

Alternatively, leave bustling La Rambla, go through a small arcade and find yourself in the quiet, stately **Plaza Real,** the city's finest square. Or simply hire a chair on the Rambla. People-watching is a cheap entertainment by any standards, and there's hoursworth to watch.

On the other side of La Rambla, the **Market of San José** is one of those classic iron structures of the 19th century. Ease your way through the throngs of bustling housewives; your ears will ring with their strident shouts. Look at the eye-catching display of Mediterranean fish, fruit and vegetables. The fish are lovingly laid out on crushed ice, as if posing for family portraits. Arc lights give an even more garish look to the fish eyes. **71**

Mounds of pig trotters (pig's feet) share the space with piles of vegetables whose names are a treat in themselves—you may be at pains to find an English equivalent.

Just beside San José Market, in the graceful Palacio de la Virreina, many an exhibition of more than local interest takes place. The palace also houses the remarkable permanent exposition of the towards the port offers, among other pleasures, an exciting shopping experience. Here, too, you can sample some of Barcelona's most celebrated eating spots.

On the other side of La Rambla, entering at the Plaza del Teatro, are the noisy streets of the infamous **Barrio Chino** ("Chinatown"). Here, while prostitution was outlawed in Spain in 1956, the colourful

Excursion boat in Barcelona port moors next to Santa María *replica.*

Colección Cambó, where each one of 50 choice works is a masterpiece.

The warren of streets to the left of La Rambla as you descend from Plaza de Cataluña

denizens of Barrio Chino's grubby bars have, one might gather, yet to be notified, and the area has a classic air of port-side low-life.

La Rambla, with its ebullience, colour and life, is the Barcelona that sticks in the mind long after the classic scenes have disappeared.

What to Do

Sports and Other Activities

Hot summers and mild winters make the Costa Brava a year-round sportsman's paradise. And with a coastline including long beaches, broad bays and scores of secluded coves, water sports are naturally the favourites. But there's plenty more to do. There are activities for everyone, ranging from the strenuous to the relaxed.

Sportsmen on the Costa Brava have one enemy: that friendly Mediterranean sun can be deceptive. If you aren't used to it, three or four hours of mid-afternoon heat can burn you a bright lobster-red. Sunburn is painful and a heavy dose can ruin a holiday, so do take the sun in easy stages—half an hour twice a day is plenty—until you have acquired some sort of tan. For the rest of the time, wear a T-shirt or something light to cover your shoulders and upper body. A hat is a good idea, too.

Here's a list of sports to choose from during a holiday on the Costa Brava:

Simple joys of sea, sun and sand are Costa Brava's priceless assets.

Boating

Most major beaches have some kind of water-craft for hire, and larger hotels fronting onto beaches may have sailing-boats available. Prices vary considerably from resort to resort.

Pedalos are two-seater craft propelled by a foot-driven waterwheel. They are equipped with a rudder and are stable enough for a young child to be aboard in the company of an adult. Two adults and one child is the usual maximum load permitted. Beach concessionaires often don't watch weather conditions. Don't take a *pedalo* out in a stiff seaward wind—you might end up in Italy!

Gondolas are flat-decked "banana-boat"-type canoes, which only provide seating for one, although two can have a lot of fun. Propulsion comes from a double-ended paddle. Gondolas tip easily, so are not suitable for younger children or non-swimmers.

Water-Skiing

Rising fuel costs mean that water-skiing is becoming an expensive way to whizz round the bay. All the more reason to double-check rival schools for length of runs, number of attempts allowed for "getting up" and discounts for multiple runs paid for in advance. Serious lessons are usually confined to the early morning, when the sea is calmest and most tourists are still in bed. For something less energetic, try powerboat parachuting. An on-shore wind, a dash of courage, and you'll be soaring heavenwards. You needn't even get your feet wet, and the view is superb.

Wind-Surfing

Wind-surfing is one of the coast's fastest-growing sports, but it's also one of the most difficult: you skim along the Mediterranean balanced on a surfboard and driven by a hand-held sail. With agility and practice and the help of an ocean breeze, you'll soon feel you're flying.

Snorkelling

An immensely popular sport in the clear waters of the Costa Brava. The rugged coastline conceals coves inaccessible except by scrambling down steep cliffs, or by boat. The basic law of snorkelling has it that the tougher the climb, the more secluded the spot, the bigger the fish—so with luck...

But there's lots of fun, too, snorkelling in quieter corners of resort beaches. In shallow water, try catching small octopus with your hands (leave them alone if you're out of your depth). You can eat them too: when you've brought one ashore, turn it inside out, pound it on a rock to soften it and dry it in the sun for 24 hours. Then slice it thinly, grill it over a charcoal fire and sprinkle it with lemon. Eat to the accompaniment of white wine.

lar—and cheapest—sport is obviously swimming. In peak season, major resort beaches are packed, but between towns you can find much less crowded strips. Catalonian beach facilities may not always be as good as in some other countries, though larger beaches have restaurants, showers and changing rooms. Beach-chairs can be hired for a daily fee.

Reasonably priced equipment is on sale in all resorts—from simple masks for children to sophisticated, high-powered spearguns for adults.

Swimming

With its long coastline, the Costa Brava's most popu-

The beach areas are usually not manned by life-guards (though some do have first-aid stations). So keep an even closer watch on children than you normally would, particularly on those rare beaches such as Playa de Pals, where there can be powerful waves. **75**

Fishing

Fishing from rocks along the coastline is popular, but results are better if you hire a boat and head for open water. Village fishermen who know local waters may be available for half-day or daily hire. You can negotiate most expeditions to include a stop at some isolated cove for a picnic lunch. The boat-owner, customarily, joins the picnic as the guest of his passengers. Cheap fishing tackle is available in most resorts.

There's abundant river fishing, also, in Gerona Province. The Rivers Ter and Oñar are well stocked with barbel, carp, tench and eel, while pike and carp are caught in Lake Bañolas. There's first-class trout fishing in government-controlled stretches along the River Segre. Licences are needed for river fishing. A special 15-day card for tourists (including trout licence) is available. Apply to ICONA (the government body concerned with wildlife preservation), General Primo de Rivera, 6, Gerona, including a passport-sized photograph and passport details.

Golf

Gerona Province offers golfers three courses:

Club de Golf de Pals, 18 holes, near Bagur.

Club de Golf Costa Brava, 18 holes, at Santa Cristina de Aro, near Playa de Aro.

Real Club de Golf de Puig-

Lush golf green in Gerona Province.

erdá, 18 holes, 3 kilometres from Puigcerdá station (in the north of the province, near the French frontier). Also has a office at: Rambla de Cataluña, 66, 3rd floor, Barcelona 7.

Horse Riding

Several ranches along the Costa Brava hire out horses.

Hunting and Shooting

Very popular amongst Catalans who bag hare, rabbit, quail, duck and partridge. For details about hunting permits and laws concerning temporary import of firearms, check with local or foreign tourist offices, or write to Servicio Nacional de Pesca Fluvial y Caza, Calle de Goya, 25, Madrid.

Skiing

Three big ski resorts are located in the Pyrenees within 100 miles of the Costa Brava: La Molina, Masella and Nuria. La Molina is the best equipped centre in Spain. It lies 20 kilometres from Puigcerdá and only 15 kilometres from the French frontier. Snow fields cover nearly 20 square miles which include 17 marked runs. The outstanding Olympic run, suited to international competition, drops more than 2,700 feet over a distance of 8,100 feet. La Molina facilities include four chair lifts, seven ski lifts, two cable cars and over a dozen hotels. Best ski months are December to April. Full information from any tourist office or from Centro de Iniciativas y Turismo del Valle de La Molina, Alp. Provincia de Gerona.

Tennis

Many hotels, apartments and villa-complexes have their own tennis courts, but due to a greater number of tennis players in summer, you may have to book a day ahead. Some hotels have professionals on staff who give lessons.

Pelota

A visit to Barcelona provides you with the chance to see this famed Basque ball-game (it's called *jai-alai* in the Basque country). Players sling the ball using wicker baskets at speeds up to 125 mph. At Palacio Frontón, Plaza del Teatro, La Rambla, Barcelona. Games daily, usually starting at 5 p.m. **77**

The Bullfight

If you've never seen a bullfight, a Costa Brava holiday provides you with the chance. You may be repelled by the spectacle, you may swear never to return to it, or you may become a lifelong *aficionado*. Whatever your reaction, you'll have to admit that the *corrida*, Spain's national fiesta, is a unique, unforgettable experience.

The fight is divided into three *tercios* (thirds), each designed to tire the animal in preparation for its death. First, the bull charges into the ring and assistants play it with capes so that the matador can examine the way it moves, the direction in which it prefers to thrust with its horns. Then he takes over and tries the bull himself, using the big red and yellow cape. This is perhaps the most beautiful part of the fight; but every graceful pass is bringing the bull closer to the inevitable finale.

The second *tercio* is when the *picador*, the mounted spearman, uses his lance on the bull's huge shoulder muscles. This spearing has two purposes: it tires the bull and it forces him to drop his head into a position which will allow the matador to place his sword for the kill. The audience invariably boos the *picador*, not for any love of the bull, but because if the spear is used too much the bull will lose his strength and will to fight. After the *picador* comes the turn of the *banderillero*, who place darts in the bull's shoulder. Lodged correctly into his muscles, the darts counter any preference the animal may have for hooking with the left or right horn.

Finally comes the third *tercio* when the matador fights the bull with the small, dark red *muleta*. Gradually he dominates the animal—even to the point where he can turn his back on it and walk casually away—and eventually comes the time known in English as "the moment of truth". With the bull theoretically completely under control, the matador sights along his sword and then lunges, leaning dangerously over the bull's horns to deliver the final thrust into a minute area between the shoulder blades.

Depending upon the quality and the bravery of the performance, the fight's *presidente* will indicate whether or not the matador is to be awarded an ear, two ears, or, after an exceptional performance, the tail of the animal he has killed. The crowd sometimes expresses its appreciation of the fight by waving handkerchiefs and tossing handbags, hats and wineskins *(botas)* into the ring.

The whole performance, consisting usually of six bulls killed by three matadors and their teams, lasts about two hours.

You may be sickened, fascinated or simply confused. A majority of foreigners are. But you will have witnessed a violent act which at times contains impressive beauty. With luck you'll begin to understand why in Spain this fantastic ballet of death is considered an art form.

On the Costa Brava, there is a choice of various bullrings: at San Feliú de Guixols, Gerona, Figueras, as well as two in Barcelona. The most outstanding performances are generally to be seen in Barcelona. Top matadors fight there in the summer, and that's where you get best value for money.

Among several seating categories at the *corrida*, a good one is *sol y sombra*, which means you'll be in sun for part of the fight and shade for the rest. Seats are bare concrete, so it's a good idea to rent a cushion. Be on time, for in this domain. Spaniards are very punctual—rarely does a bullfight start late.

Tickets purchased in advance—those ordered through your hotel, for instance—cost 20 per cent more than the box-office price on the day of the fight. But the surcharge is worth the saving in queuing time, and tickets sold by street-hawkers are exorbitantly expensive.

Flamenco

Flamenco was born in Andalusia, in southern Spain, and that region remains the stronghold of the art. But in Barcelona and the bigger resort towns, you'll be able to visit a *tablao*—a floor show featuring guitar players, singers and dancers that at least gives something of the feel of flamenco—during your Costa Brava holiday. Flamenco is said to be Moorish in its origins, and certainly there's a resemblance to the wailing chants typical of Arab music.

There are two main groups of flamenco songs. One, bouncier and more cheerful, is the *cante chico* ("light song"). *Fandangos, sevillanas, bulerías, alegrías, malagueñas*—these are all part of the *cante chico*. *Cante chico* themes are light, but they can also be touching.

The second group of songs is the *cante jondo* ("deep song"). Slow, piercing, nearly always brutally emotional, it deals with the intricacies and torments of love, death, the whole human predicament. It is the song of the great flamenco singers.

But you are highly unlikely to encounter any genuine *cante jondo,* although recordings abound; it's *cante chico* you'll hear at the *tablao flamenco*. These shows, which usually include a drink and a certain amount of audience participation, are staged in many tourist resorts.

The Sardana

The energetic yet graceful national dance of Catalonia, the *sardana,* with its haunting woodwind accompaniment, hypnotizes Catalans wherever they may be. The exact origins of this disciplined ring dance are unknown. But in the *Iliad,* Homer describes a Greek dance very like the *sardana,* and researchers suggest that Greeks may have introduced it to Catalonia when they were established in Ampurias and elsewhere on the coast.

The modern *sardana* existed by the end of the 18th century, and in the 19th was revived after enthusiastic work by an Andalusian who lived in Figueras—José "Pep" Ventura. Amongst *aficionados* he's called Pep of the *tenora,* an allusion to a strident clarinet-like instrument played by the 11-man *cobla,* or band.

The deceptively simple-looking *sardana* is danced in normal everyday clothes, except on special occasions, and very often Catalans simply put their satchels, bags or briefcases in the centre of the circle. The dancers form a circle which grows as newcomers join it. If it proves unwieldy, they simply form another. If they run out of room, they make circles within circles. Each group has a leader who keeps meticulous time and signals changes. If he makes one error his ring loses its rhythm and can't complete the final step in time with the band.

er; long-haired students join the same circle as middle-aged housewives. They may have little in common in everyday life, but the *sardana* reminds them that, whatever their social differences, they are Catalans. Even tourists can, technically, join in. In actual fact, prudence is advisable. There is a fairly strict rule that puts an end to most tourists' ambitions: no local would

and can't complete the final step in time with the band.

The wonder of the *sardana,* quickly noted by visitors, is the spirit it generates. The dance—performed in many resorts on weekend evenings—cuts all barriers. Doctors and farmers dance together, the whole scene.

Social barriers melt as Catalan national dance, sardana, *starts up.*

ever dare move into a circle that has a much higher standard of dancing than he is capable of, and the uninitiated visitor might thus find himself edged out. **81**

Shopping

Shopping Hours

Most Catalan shops are open from 9 a.m. to 1 p.m., and again from 4 to 8 p.m. The hours between 1–4 p.m. are devoted to lunch and that most venerable of Spanish customs, the *siesta*. This, however, does not apply to the department stores, and for those not wishing or able to have a rest, it can be the least tiring moment to wander round these stores. In summer, shops in tourist resorts often stay open until 8.30 p.m. Bars and cafés are generally open without a break from 8 a.m. to midnight or later.

Best Buys

Perhaps the best buy in Spain today is footwear. Shoes and boots, both men's and women's, are of good quality leather. Though fashionable models are expensive, you can find bargains in everyday styles. (Shoes for children, though, can be more expensive than elsewhere.)

Items in leather and suede (sports jackets, full-length coats, handbags, etc.) remain among the best buys, but prices are rising.

Seasoned travellers know all about Spanish leather; but few realize that Spanish high fashion *(alta costura)* is slowly but surely edging in on the international market. Your resort boutique may not have much to offer in fashions, but in Barcelona, watch out for the big names.

While window-shopping on the Costa Brava, you may notice the high quality of children's clothing—and the unexpectedly high prices. If you want to dress your children like royalty, and can afford it, Spain is the place to buy.

Spirits and cigarettes are still a bargain by European and American standards. Top foreign-brand drinks, produced under licence in Spain, are sold for less than they cost at home; locally made cigarettes are also good value for money; a full range of imported Cuban cigars is available at prices considerably lower than in England, while quality Canary Island cigars are even cheaper.

Locally produced pottery and ceramics, colourful and decorative, or just utilitarian, make interesting gifts. Most resorts have at least one pottery shop, and some resorts are visited by salesmen leading donkeys laden with jugs and vases. Bargaining is acceptable with the latter.

Souvenirs

Thirty million tourists visit Spain annually (one to every Spaniard) and the souvenir industry strains to give them something new to buy. Most people, however, stick to the "traditional" Spanish souvenirs, such as bullfight posters (with or without your own name printed), bullfight swords, inlaid chess-sets, replicas of classic swords and pistols produced in Toledo, wrought-iron work or the typical Spanish *bota,* the soft leather wineskin.

More useful items, produced for local consumption as well as the tourist trade, are hand-made shawls, embroidered linen, lace-work, painted fans, hand-woven shopping baskets and many other items made of wickerwork and wood. Many of these objects are the work of craftsmen who, even in the face of Spain's recent dramatic entry into the 20th century, still pursue the age-old techniques of their fathers. (Industrialization only reached Spain with real force about 30 years ago.) But time's short…

Antiques

If you know what to look for, worthwhile antiques can be bought at bargain prices in Spain. You'll find antique shops in most larger resorts as well as in Gerona, Barcelona and Besalú; but once an antique is inside a shop, the price goes skyhigh. Stroll through the streets by Barcelona Cathedral and the triangle formed by Calle de Puer-

Shopping anywhere in Spain is a happy venture for bargain-hunters. **83**

taferriso, Calle de Petrilxol, Calle del Pino. Search, too, at the weekly outdoor markets held in most villages and towns. Sometimes, gypsies come in from the country with interesting, if battered, odds and ends for sale. You may find hand-carved wooden bowls, heavy iron keys, wrought-iron work, brightly painted tiles and, occasionally, tattered paintings and

Fresh Mediterranean produce fills fruit-and-vegetable market stalls.

prints (which just might be worth something).

The flea market in Barcelona is at the end of Paseo del Dos de Mayo, near Plaza de las Glorias.

Where to Shop

Tourist centres may look like shopping paradises, but they rarely are. Some shops are excellent, but most tend to carry only lines with a proven turnover, so your choice is limited. And, in resort areas, prices are liable to be high.

So where should one shop? It's worthwhile keeping expensive purchases for a visit to Gerona, Barcelona or larger inland towns. There you may get really excited by what you see, and you'll save 10, even 20 per cent, with a far wider choice. But, if you can't make it to one of the larger towns, don't worry; your resort, however small, will almost certainly be capable of supplying last-minute traditional buys or afterthoughts.

Although designed for tourists, the Pueblo Español in Barcelona is a good place to pick up inventively designed objects, such as wickerwork baskets, carpets and bedspreads, as well as souvenirs at reasonable prices.

Shopping Tips

Wherever you shop, try to compare prices of items in at least three stores before buying. Price control in Spain hasn't reached the sophisticated level of other countries. It's very much an open market, with few shops using the price-slashing ploy. And don't presume that because a shop is bigger its prices will be lower; one shop may blatantly overcharge, while the neighbouring store is perfectly honest. Always ask for a discount *(un descuento, una rebaja)* when spending more than 1,000 pesetas. Sometimes you get it.

Requesting a discount is standard shopping practice, but haggling is not. Save that for antique shops and outdoor markets (though never at food stalls). Hard bargaining with gypsies is not only acceptable but essential to financial survival.

If you're charged an extra peseta or two for a packet of cigarettes bought from a *quiosco* (street kiosk), street-corner salesman, bar, café or restaurant, don't think you're being cheated. These people buy from official tobacco shops *(tabacaleras,* which also sell postage stamps) and raise the price to make a small, government-approved profit.

To Market, To Market!

Market-day may be a world-wide custom; in the Mediterranean setting, however, it always has something quite special about it, and no less so in Catalonia. For the Catalans, market-day, whether it be the daily food mart or the weekly clothes and general market, is a time to buy and sell, a chance to gossip, an excuse to down a *copita* (glass) of sherry with friends. Even the most modest daily markets are an institution, a social occasion, an essential part of communal life.

Here's a list of market-days for main Costa Brava towns:

Monday: Blanes, Cadaqués, Torroella de Montgrí.

Tuesday: Lloret de Mar, Besalú, Caldas de Malavella, Castelló de Ampurias, Palamós.

Wednesday: Bañolas, Llansá.

Thursday: Tossa de Mar, Estartit, Figueras, Llagostera.

Friday: La Bisbal, Puerto de la Selva.

Saturday: Gerona.

Sunday: La Escala, Palafrugell, Rosas, San Feliú de Guixols, Tordera (Barcelona Province).

Ferias and Festivals

Spain is the land of the *fiesta,* and the Costa Brava has its share of both religious and folk festivals. Information about exact dates and times of fiestas in your area can be requested at town halls or tourist offices. At tourist offices, ask for a copy of the "Spanish Tourist Calendar" booklet for Gerona Province (to cover Spain, there are nine volumes), which lists all fiestas on the Costa Brava. Here are some outstanding annual events:

February
La Molina: Skiing championships.

March
In most larger towns: Holy Week observances. At its most spectacular in Gerona, but more modest processions in other towns. Some villages present the Dance of Death when villagers dressed as skeletons dance to drum-beats. Other towns perform a Passion play, notably in Verges.

April
Figueras: Town fair, including an agricultural and industrial display, art exhibitions, bullfights and a flower battle.

May
Gerona: Provincial flower show held in the beautiful cloisters of San Pedro de Galligans Church, which houses the Archaeological Museum.

Ripoll: Town fair in honour of San Eudaldo. Dancing, cultural events and sports.

June
Palamós: Annual town fair, featuring folkloric and sports events.

San Pedro Pescador: Events include water-skiing on the river and *sardana* dancing.

Tossa de Mar: Local fair featuring folkloric events.

July
Olot: An *aplec* (or reunion) of *sardana* dancers. Some 5,000 participants, including French Catalans, dance the *sardana* almost non-stop until well after midnight.

Calonge: Annual music festival.

Estartit, Palamós: Annual religious festivals, including a seaborne procession, fishing competitions, *sardana* dancing.

Lloret de Mar: The famous annual fair in honour of St. Christine (see p. 50). Fishing boats sail from Lloret to the beach beneath Santa Cristina Chapel. On the way, a wreath is thrown overboard in memory of those who have died at sea. The two-day festival includes folk dancing and has been declared of special interest to tourists.

Santa Cristina de Aro, Blanes, Port Bou, San Feliú de Guixols, Estartit: Annual fairs including *sardana* dancing.

Cadaqués: Annual International Festival of Music and Painting.

Castillo de Aro: Annual Music Festival.

August

Pals: Festival of San Domingo, featuring *sardana* dancing.

Puerto de la Selva: Local celebrations with *sardana* dancing and water-skiing contests.

Playa de Aro: Folkloric festival.

San Feliú de Guixols: Major festival with folk dancing, sports and cultural events, bullfights, fireworks and prizes for the best sandcastles and sculptures made on the beach.

Torroella de Montgrí: Local festival with *sardana* dancing.

Llansá: Sardana and other folkloric dances as part of the local fair.

September

La Escala: Local festivities, including the *sardana.*

Cadaqués: Local fair; *sardanas* and sports events.

Lloret de Mar: Local rural festival.

October

San Feliú de Guixols: "Day of the Sea". Marine processions and *sardana* dancing.

Gerona: Festival of San Narciso. Includes bullfights and horse shows.

November

Torroella de Montgrí: Festivities in honour of Santa Catalina. Includes *sardana* dancing.

Other Possibilities

Barbecues

Check at your hotel desk or at travel agencies to see if there's a barbecue *(barbacoa)* in your area—announcements of such events are usually posted on boards outside. For an all-in price, you can eat and drink as much as you like and, if you are still capable, dance. This is a good occasion for getting to know other like-minded visitors to the Costa Brava. Transport is provided.

Boat Trips

You can take boat trips from the beaches at most major Costa Brava resorts. Some last only an hour, others take you to a destination where you enjoy a picnic lunch before returning home. You'll be impressed by the dramatic sight of the Costa Brava coastline. The boats beach right on the sand, while swimmers clear the way.

Films

Most films are dubbed into Spanish. But in Gerona and Barcelona some cinemas show films in original-language versions. Consult the entertainment sections of local newspapers for programmes.

Casino Gambling

After four decades of prohibition, casino gambling has been legalized in Spain. Casinos charge a small entrance fee and restrict admission to holders of an identity card or passport. Casinos on the coast include Casino de Lloret de Mar, Hotel Montecristo (Gerona) and Castle of Perelada Casino.

Galleries and Museums

Several Costa Brava resorts have small museums which are mentioned in the WHERE TO Go section. Listed here are the more important museums or galleries in the province.

Figueras

Museo del Ampurdán (Ampurdán Museum) on the main square. Dedicated to the history and other aspects of the region. Well organized.

Teatro-Museo Dalí (Dalí Theatre-Museum). A museum as eccentric as its founder. Many works by Salvador Dalí in all mediums.

Ampurias

Museo Arqueológico (Archaeological Museum). Large collection of Greek and Roman objects found on the site right beside the museum.

Gerona

Museo Arqueológico (Archaeological Museum) in San Pedro de Galligans Church. Greek and Roman objects excavated at Ampurias and some excellent paintings (Tintoretto, Murillo).

Museo Histórico de la Ciudad (Museum of City History) in Calle de la Forsa. Documents and objects relating to Gerona's history.

Museo de la Catedral (Cathedral Museum) in the cathedral chapter-house. Among many interesting exhibits, two are outstanding: a 10th-century illuminated manuscript *(Book of the Apocalypse)* and a 12th-century tapestry.

Salvador Dali's museum in Figueras arouses many a heated debate.

Ripoll

Museo de Arte Pirenaico (Museum of Pyrenean Folklore) beside the monastery in the centre of town. Remarkable collection of tools, clothing and household implements relating to country life. Also excellent collection of old handguns.

89

Wining and Dining

The Catalans appreciate hearty dishes based on honest ingredients fresh from the farm—and the sea. If you share this enthusiasm, some memorable treats are in store.

But to find native cooking, you'll have to escape from the tourist hotels, where the food tends towards a bland international compromise. Break the protective shield and sniff out the real places where the Catalans themselves are to be found.*

Since the Mediterranean is near at hand, the accent is on fish. Here are some traditional species you'll be offered—normally fried or simply grilled and served without a sauce. A tomato, onion and lettuce salad is usually offered as an optional side dish:

Lenguado—sole; *mero*—sea bass; *salmonetes*—Mediterranean red mullet; *calama-*

Dining under the ramparts of Tossa.

res—squid; *gambas*—prawns (shrimp); *langosta*—spiny lobster (seasonal and always expensive).

Two classic Spanish dishes, as popular in Catalonia as elsewhere, are *paella* and *gazpacho*.

Gazpacho is a tangy chilled soup made with tomatoes, green peppers, cucumbers, onions, croutons, oil, vinegar and spices. Many of the ingredients are served on the side and may be added to taste. It's been aptly described as "liquid salad" and makes an ideal first course to a fish dinner.

Paella, the best-known of all Spanish dishes, usually combines seafood and chicken, pork or rabbit, served on a base of saffron-coloured rice; peas, red peppers and anything else that takes the cook's fancy are also included. Normally served at lunchtime, the best *paellas* are always cooked to order, a process that takes at least half an hour.

But Catalonia has plenty of specialities of its own, e.g.:

A *zarzuela* is the Spanish version of an operetta, or musical comedy, and like a light-hearted musical, the dish of the same name offers a little of everything. It's a triumphant concoction of up to a dozen different kinds of seafood, including prawns, shrimp and clams, octopus, squid and various white fish, all topped by a brandy-and-wine sauce. It's mouth-watering, and filling.

Pollastre amb xamfaina: casseroled chicken served with an aubergine-and-tomato stew.

Butifarra: a rich, delicious pork sausage. It may come with chips and/or other vegetables, with eggs, or even an omelette, when it's called *tortilla ampurdanesa.*

Habas a la Catalana: broadbeans cooked with ham and *butifarra.* Sometimes only the broadbeans and ham are served, in which case the dish is eaten as an entrée.

The pastries of the Costa Brava will destroy your diet. Just look in a bakery window; you don't have to know the names of all the *tartas.* One is more delectable than the next, crowned with nuts, custard, dried fruits, meringue, chocolate or powdered sugar.

Crema catalana: a custard with a crisp, caramel-glaze topping.

* For more information on wining and dining in Spain, consult the Berlitz EUROPEAN MENU READER.

Restaurants

Spanish restaurants are officially graded by forks—one fork for the lowest grade, five forks for the top. But forks are awarded according to facilities available and the length of the menu, neither of which has anything to do with quality of the food. On the whole, three- and four-fork restaurants do serve good food, but two-fork establishments have a reputation amongst Spanish gourmets for giving excellent value.

By law, all restaurants must offer a *plato del día* (day's special or set menu). This is usually three courses with bread and wine at a stated price which depends on the restaurant's rating. Most set menu and *à la carte* prices include service, but in Spain a small tip is customary: 10 per cent is normally adequate. For more specific tipping recommendations, see pp. 121–122 in the Blueprint section.

Most restaurants on the coast are open for lunch from 1–3 p.m. Dinner is normally served from 8 until 10 p.m. (or even later in larger towns).

A hint to keep costs down: order *vino de la casa* (house wine). You'll save half or two-thirds over the price of a bottled wine.

Beach Restaurants
(*Merenderos*)

Beach restaurants are scattered along the Costa Brava, and if you can't face returning to your hotel or are determined to spend the whole day at the beach, it's hard to beat them for convenience and atmosphere. Informality is the keyword; the waitress is as likely to be wearing a bikini as the customer. Menus are simple, but tasty and filling: *paella,* fish, omelette and the ubiquitous steak or chicken.

Bars and Cafés

These establishments are indispensable to the Spanish lifestyle. It has been suggested that if bars and cafés were suddenly to disappear, the Spanish economy would grind to a halt. It certainly does seem that more bright ideas are launched, more partnerships formed, more deals clinched in cafés than in offices.

Some cafés open at crack of dawn, catering to early-morning workers; most are open by 8.30 a.m. to serve breakfast. One of the pleasures of the Mediterranean is drinking an early-morning *café con leche* (white coffee) at an outdoor café while a town comes to life. The price of a coffee buys a seat at a table for as long as you care to stay.

Wines and spirits are served at all hours in Spanish bars and cafés. Bills include service, but small tips are customary. It's usually 10–15 per cent cheaper to take your coffee or aperitif standing at the bar.

The patrons at this typical open-air local café take their time as they catch up on the latest news.

Tapas

Tapas have been called Spain's greatest contribution to the world of food. A *tapa* is a bite-sized morsel: meat-balls, olives, fried fish, other sea-food, vegetable salad, mush-rooms grilled, then dipped in garlic sauce...a *tapa* can be almost anything.

The term derives from the old custom of giving a bite of food with a drink, the snack

Fishermen unload their day's haul, meaning fresh seafood at the table.

being served on a saucer (*tapa* means literally "lid") which covered the glass. Today, sadly, the custom of giving the *tapa* is all but dead, though the idea of selling it is stronger than ever. Some bars specialize in *tapas,* so instead of dining formally in a restaurant, you can fill up in a bar by eating your way down a long counter crammed with tastily prepared dishes. (Vocabulary: *una tapa* is the bite-sized portion; *una ración* is half a plateful; and *una porción* is a large helping.) But beware: you could end up spending more for a feast of *tapas* than for a conventional meal.

Wines and Spirits

The most famous of all Spanish wines is sherry, a wine fortified with brandy, which is matured and bottled in the Andalusian town of Jerez de la Frontera. There are five main types: *manzanilla,* very pale, light to the taste and dry; *fino,* also very pale but slightly heavier; *amontillado,* amber-coloured, medium-dry; *oloroso,* dark gold in colour and with a fuller body; *cream,* sweet, smooth and the most popular of all sherries.

Spanish table wines range from adequate to excellent. For cheaper wines, try those from Valdepeñas in central Spain. Many towns in Gerona Province produce *vino corriente* (ordinary wine), as do some of the resort towns (Llansá's wines are highly considered). Perhaps the best of all

Geronese wines are those produced in the privately owned castle in Perelada; outstanding is *claustro,* a sparkling wine which experts claim is on a par with *gran codorniu* (produced in the Catalan town of San Sadurní de Noya). Other high-quality Spanish wines are the well-known reds from Rioja and Logroño.

Spanish brandy can be a bit heavy and sweet, and takes some getting used to. However, there are infinite varieties and *aficionados* swear by it. It is always bargain-priced.

Spain is a bonanza for drinkers of all categories. Most brands of spirits are produced under licence in the country and remain inexpensive, despite recent price increases. Imported Scotch whisky is an outstanding exception. Locally produced whisky tends to leave connoisseurs unenthusiastic.

Sangría, the popular summer drink, is a mixture of red wine, lemonade, brandy and chopped fruit. Spaniards drink it in moderation as a refresher. Tourists who take it with their meals may find it

too heavy and strong; ask to have it diluted with soda-water.

Breakfast
This comes last, because in Spain breakfast is such an insignificant meal, just an eye-opener to keep one alive until a huge and late lunch. A typical Costa Brava breakfast consists of a cup of coffee and past-

Outdoor cafés and restaurants are a focal point of Spain's social life.

ry. Breakfast coffee (*café con leche*) is half coffee, half hot milk. If it tastes too foreign to you, many bars and restaurants stock milder instant coffee as well. Also, in deference to foreign habits, *desayuno completo* is now available in most hotels and some cafés: orange juice, eggs, toast and coffee.

Returning to the subject of breakfast pastry, two types are worth a try. *Ensaimadas*, large fluffy sweet rolls dusted with sugar, are a breakfast idea from the Costa Brava's overseas cousins, the Balearic Islanders. If you can find them, don't miss trying *churros*. *Churros* are fritters, often made before your eyes by a contraption which shoots the batter into boiling oil. If you *don't* dunk *churros* in your coffee, everyone will stare. *Churros* served with a very thick, hot chocolate is also a very popular afternoon snack in Spain.

To Help You Order...

Could we have a table?	**¿Nos puede dar una mesa?**
Do you have a set menu?	**¿Tiene un menú del día?**
I'd like a/an/some...	**Quisiera...**

beer	**una cerveza**	milk	**leche**
bread	**pan**	mineral water	**agua mineral**
coffee	**un café**	napkin	**una servilleta**
condiments	**los condimentos**	potatoes	**patatas**
cutlery	**los cubiertos**	rice	**arroz**
dessert	**un postre**	salad	**una ensalada**
fish	**pescado**	sandwich	**un bocadillo**
fruit	**fruta**	soup	**una sopa**
glass	**un vaso**	sugar	**azúcar**
ice-cream	**un helado**	tea	**un té**
meat	**carne**	(iced) water	**agua (fresca)**
menu	**la carta**	wine	**vino**

...and Read the Menu

aceitunas	olives	guisantes	peas
ajo	garlic	helado	ice-cream
albaricoques	apricots	higos	figs
albóndigas	meatballs	huevos	eggs
almejas	baby clams	jamón	ham
anchoas	anchovies	judías	beans
anguila	eel	langosta	spiny lobster
arroz	rice	langostino	prawn
asado	roast	lenguado	sole
atún	tunny (tuna)	limón	lemon
bacalao	codfish	lomo	loin
besugo	sea bream	manzana	apple
bistec	beefsteak	mariscos	shellfish
boquerones	fresh anchovies	mejillones	mussels
caballa	mackerel	melocotón	peach
calamares	squid	merluza	hake
(a la romana)	(deep fried)	naranja	orange
callos	tripe	ostras	oysters
cangrejo	crab	pastel	cake
caracoles	snails	pescado	fish
cebollas	onions	pescadilla	whiting
cerdo	pork	pez espada	swordfish
champiñones	mushrooms	pimiento	green pepper
chorizo	a spicy pork	piña	pineapple
	sausage	plátano	banana
chuleta	chops	pollo	chicken
cordero	lamb	postre	dessert
dorada	sea-bass	pulpitos	baby octopus
ensalada	salad	queso	cheese
entremeses	hors-d'oeuvre	salchichón	salami
estofado	stew	salmonete	red mullet
filete	fillet	salsa	sauce
flan	caramel mould	sandía	watermelon
frambuesas	raspberries	sopa	soup
fresas	strawberries	ternera	veal
frito	fried	tortilla	omelet
galletas	biscuits	tostada	toast
	(cookies)	trucha	trout
gambas	shrimp	uvas	grapes
granadas	pomegranates	verduras	vegetables

97

How to Get There

If the choice of ways to go is bewildering, the complexity of fares and regulations can be downright stupefying. A reliable travel agent can suggest which plan is best for your timetable and budget.

BY AIR

Scheduled Flights

From the U.K.: There are regular, direct, non-stop scheduled services from London to Gerona, the most convenient airport for resorts on the Costa Brava, and also numerous flights to the area's main airport, Barcelona, from both London and Dublin.

Remember that if you are prepared to travel at night on certain days of the week—and stay for at least six days—you may be entitled to reductions of as much as 44 per cent on the normal scheduled fare, a worthwhile saving for those who need to be budget-conscious.

Scheduled airlines also offer reduced excursion fares to youths under 21 and students under 26.

From North America: All major North American airports are linked with Barcelona by frequent service via Madrid, Paris or other European gateways.

If you can plan—and pay—far enough in advance, APEX (Advance Purchase Excursion) fares mean considerable savings on most scheduled flights.

Charter Flights and Package Tours

From the British Isles: Following a series of bankruptcies and other difficulties, most British tour operators now offer guarantees on their arrangements, though last-minute surcharges are often imposed.

On the whole, however, the all-in package—flight, hotel and board included—remains good value. Read your contract carefully before signing. Most travel agents recommend cancellation insurance, a modestly priced safeguard; you lose no money if illness or accident force you to cancel your holiday.

From North America: Group-affinity charters require you to have belonged to the organization sponsoring a flight for at least six months before departure.

However, the U.S. Civil Aeronautics Board (CAB) is greatly liberalising regulations governing charter flights. Under new rules, travel agents can offer OTC (One-Stop Inclusive-Tour Charter), a package that includes specific hotel and other ground arrangements. This type of package isn't always available for a particular destination, but if you can find one available to Barcelona or elsewhere in Spain, you'll save a great deal in comparison with APEX or regular airline tickets and independently arranged accommodation.

Student flights: An extensive charter network for students, operating throughout Europe, includes flights to Barcelona and Gerona from Britain and other countries. National or on-campus student travel offices will have details.

BY CAR

By car ferry: The principal cross-Channel routes link Southern England with France.

The route through Paris is almost entirely toll motorway (expressway) to the Spanish border. The Spanish motorway, the *Autopista del Mediterráneo*, now runs to Alicante.

BY RAIL

Good though crowded trains link Spain with Great Britain. For any long trip, sleeper reservations are recommended. Passengers will have to change trains at the Spanish border, as the Spanish tracks have a wider gauge than those on most of the Continent. The only exception is the Trans-Europ Express, which has adjustable axles.

Once in Spain, the main railway service in the Costa Brava region starts at Port Bou, near the frontier with France, and then heads southwards to Barcelona. Several motorcoach lines link the railway stations of Figueras, Flassá, Gerona, Caldas de Malavella with Blanes and other important towns and resorts on the Costa Brava.

Eurailpass: North Americans—in fact anyone except residents of Europe—can travel on a flat-rate, unlimited mileage ticket, valid for first-class rail travel anywhere in Western Europe outside of Great Britain. But you must sign up before you leave home.

Student-railpass: The same system, with cheaper second-class accommodation for two months. Only full-time students under 26 are eligible.

When to Go

From November through March—darkest winter in much of Europe—shirtsleeve sunshine is still to be found on the Costa Brava, with temperatures usually in the upper 50s (Fahrenheit) and seldom falling below the mid-40s.

Nevertheless, the normally balmy days may be interrupted by chill winds and that rare local phenomenon—rain.

From June to September, hot days with low humidity are only occasionally broken by cooler evenings. In March, April, May and October, temperatures are usually quite warm, and these are probably the best months for a Costa Brava visit, if you want to get away from the crowds.

		J	F	M	A	M	J	J	A	S	O	N	D
Air temperature (maximum)	F	55	57	63	66	73	79	86	84	79	70	63	55
	C	13	14	17	19	23	26	30	29	26	21	17	13
Air temperature (minimum)	F	36	37	41	46	52	59	63	63	59	52	43	37
	C	2	3	5	8	11	15	17	17	15	11	6	3
Sea temperature	F	55	55	55	57	61	68	72	73	72	68	61	57
	C	13	13	13	14	16	20	22	23	22	20	16	14
Hours of sunshine		147	164	184	205	245	255	302	262	206	178	159	137

All figures shown are approximate monthly averages.

Planning Your Budget

To give you an idea of what to expect, here are some average prices in Spanish pesetas. Remember that all prices must be regarded as approximate and that inflation is running high.

Baby-Sitters: around 150–200 ptas. per hour.

Camping: 150 ptas. per person per day plus 100 ptas. for tent, 200 ptas. for car/caravan.

Car Hire: *Seat 127* 1,100 ptas. per day, 10 ptas. per km., 15,500 ptas. per week (unlimited mileage); *Seat 124 D* 1,400 ptas. per day, 13 ptas. per km., 20,000 ptas. per week (unlimited mileage); *Seat 132* 3,000 ptas. per day, 27 ptas. per km., 46,000 ptas. per week (unlimited mileage).

Cigarettes: Spanish brands 25–50 ptas., imported 80 ptas. and up.

Entertainment: *cinema* 80–150 ptas., *flamenco nightclub* 600 ptas., *bullfight* 1,000 ptas., *discotheque* 150–500 ptas.

Guides and Interpreters: 1,500 ptas. half day, 6,000 ptas. full day.

Hairdressers and Barbers: *man's* haircut 400 ptas.; *woman's* haircut 300 ptas., shampoo and set 450 ptas., blow-dry 500 ptas., permanent wave 800–1,000 ptas.

Hotels (double room with bath, high season, averages): ***** 7,000 ptas., **** 3,500 ptas., *** 2,000 ptas., ** 1,000 ptas., * 800 ptas.

Meals and Drinks: *Continental breakfast* 125–200 ptas., *lunch/dinner* in fairly good establishment 800–1,000 ptas., *coffee* 30 ptas., *brandy* (Spanish) 80 ptas., *beer/soft drinks* 30–50 ptas.

Shopping Bag: *loaf of bread* 30 ptas., *butter* (250 g.) 130 ptas., *eggs* (per dozen) 100 ptas., *beefsteak* (½ kg.) 350 ptas., *coffee* (250 g.) 200 ptas., *fruit juice* (per litre) 80 ptas., *wine* (bottle) 60–90 ptas.

Sports: *water-skiing* 400–600 ptas. for 10 min., half-hour lesson 1,000 ptas.; *horseriding* 500 ptas. per hour; *tennis court* fee 300 ptas. per hour, instruction from 700 ptas. per hour; *golf* (per day) green fee 800–1,000 ptas., caddie fee 1,000 ptas.

Taxi: initial charge 30 ptas., plus 15 ptas. per km.

BLUEPRINT for a Perfect Trip

An A-Z Summary of Practical Information and Facts

A star (*) following an entry indicates that relevant prices are to be found on page 101.

Listed after some basic entries is the appropriate Spanish translation, usually in the singular, plus a number of phrases that should help you when seeking assistance.

All information given here, including prices on page 101, has been carefully checked. But if the reader should come across any errors or changes, we would be glad to hear of them.

AIRPORT *(aeropuerto)*. The Costa Brava is served by Gerona airport, 11 kilometres from the provincial capital of Gerona. At the time of writing, there is a post office and telegram service, but no tourist office, porters or bus service. (Tourists arriving by charter flights are, of course, met by agency buses.) Taxis from the airport to Gerona take about 20 minutes. From Gerona there are bus services to all Costa Brava resorts.

Travellers on scheduled international flights arrive at Barcelona airport, well supplied with porters, currency-exchange offices, a tourist information office and car-hire firms. A bus service links the airport with central Barcelona.

Porter!	**¡Mozo!**
Taxi!	**¡Taxi!**
Where's the bus for …?	**¿De dónde sale el autobús para …?**

BABY-SITTERS* *(señorita para cuidar niños)*. This service can usually be arranged by your hotel. Rates can vary considerably but are generally lower in the quieter resort areas; in most places charges go up after midnight.

Can you get me a baby-sitter for tonight?	**¿Puede conseguirme una señorita para cuidar los niños esta noche?**

CAMPING*. The Costa Brava is extremely popular with campers, and there are nearly 100 official sites dotted up and down the length of the coast and inland where campers can pitch their tents.

Facilities vary, but most sites have electricity and running water. Many have shops and children's playgrounds, and some boast launderettes and restaurants. Rates depend to a large extent on the facilities available.

For a complete list of campsites, consult any Spanish National Tourist Office (see TOURIST INFORMATION OFFICES), or write to Agrupación Nacional de Campings de España (ANCE):

Duque de Medinaceli, 2, Madrid.

May we camp here?	**¿Podemos acampar aquí?**
We have a tent/caravan (trailer).	**Tenemos una tienda de camping/ una caravana.**

C   **CAR HIRE★** *(coches de alquiler)*. See also DRIVING. There are car hire firms in most tourist resorts and main towns. The most common type of car for hire is the Seat, the Spanish version of the Italian Fiat available in several models.

Unless payment is made with a major credit card, a deposit, as well as advance payment of the estimated rental charge, is generally required. A tax of 2.7% is added to the total bill. Third-party insurance is automatically included.

Normally you must be over 21 and hold an international driving licence. In practice, British, American and European licences are accepted in almost all situations.

I'd like to rent a car tomorrow.	**Quisiera alquilar un coche para mañana.**
for one day/a week	**por un día/una semana**
Please include full insurance coverage.	**Haga el favor de incluir el seguro todo riesgo.**

CIGARETTES, CIGARS, TOBACCO★ *(cigarrillos, puros, tabaco)*. Most Spanish cigarettes are made of strong black tobacco and have a high nicotine content.

Ducados are popular for filtered black tobacco; *Un-X-Dos* (filter) and *Bisonte* (non-filter) are similar to foreign light brands. Nearly all popular foreign makes are available at twice to three times the price of the domestic product.

Locally made cigars are passable and cheap; among the better cigars, those from the Canary islands are excellent. Cuban cigars are available nearly everywhere. Most visitors to Spain consider local pipe tobacco a little rough.

A packet of cigarettes/matches.	**Un paquete de cigarrillos/fósforos.**
filter-tipped	**con filtro**
without filter	**sin filtro**
light tobacco	**tabaco rubio**
dark tobacco	**tabaco negro**

CLOTHING. From June to September the days are always hot, but evenings sometimes turn cool, so take a jacket or cardigan. During the rest of the year evenings are often chilly, and an unseasonably cold wind, the *tramontana*, can upset the benign climate, particularly in the northern part of the Costa Brava.

The days are long gone when Spanish authorities banned bikinis and made men wear bathing-suit tops. Spanish girls are as much at home in bikinis on the beach now as the foreigners. Topless bathing, too, is quite common on some stretches of beach. In spite of the upheaval in Spain since General Franco's death, and the general realignment of attitudes, fundamental codes of behaviour change slowly, and discretion should be used as to when and where topless bathing is practised.

Going to and from the beach, men are expected to slip on a shirt, and women, an informal dress.

More sober clothing—no shorts or miniskirts—should, of course, be worn when visiting churches.

Will I need a jacket and tie?	**¿Necesito chaqueta y corbata?**
Is it all right if I wear this?	**¿Voy bien así?**

COMMUNICATION

Post offices are for mail and telegrams only; normally you can't make telephone calls from them.

Hours vary slightly from town to town, but routine postal business is generally transacted: from 9 a.m. to 1 or 1.30 p.m. and 4 to 6 or 7 p.m., Monday to Saturday except for Saturday afternoons.

Postage stamps *(sello)* are also on sale at tobacconists' *(tabacalera* or *estanco)* and often at hotel desks.

If you see a mailbox marked *extranjero,* it's for foreign-destination mail.

Poste restante (general delivery): If you don't know in advance where you'll be staying, you can have your mail addressed to *Lista de correos* (poste restante or general delivery) in the nearest town:

> Mr. John Smith
> Lista de correos
> Palamós
> Spain

Take your passport to the post office as identification.

Telegrams: Usual hours for telegrams: 8 a.m.–midnight. The main telegraph office in Gerona:

Avenida Ramón Folch; tel.: 20 18 40 and 20 22 96 is open 24 hours a day.

Your hotel receptionist will also handle telegrams for you.

Night letters or night-rate telegrams *(telegrama de noche)* are delivered the following morning and cost much less than straight-rate messages.

Telephone. The telephone office is almost always independent of the local post office. It is identified by a blue and white sign. Major towns and many tourist centres have automatic dialling facilities for local, inter-urban and some international calls. Area, or STD, code numbers are given in the telephone directory. In smaller towns and villages, however, where the phones are not yet automatic, you'll have to go through the operator.

Telephone booths, once almost non-existent in Spain, are now being installed in increasing numbers. You'll need a supply of coins to use them; a 5-peseta coin for some newer call boxes, three 1-peseta coins for the older public phones. You may come across a coin box which requires *una ficha* (a token), which can be bought for 3 pesetas at a café.

The charges are totalled on a meter hidden from your view. If you think you have been overcharged, you are entitled to a receipt for the cost of the call.

To reverse the charges, ask for *cobro revertido*. For a personal (person-to-person) call, specify *persona a persona*.

Where is the (nearest) post office?	**¿Dónde está la oficina de correos más cercana?**
Have you received any mail for …?	**¿Ha recibido correo para …?**
A stamp for this letter/postcard, please.	**Por favor, un sello para esta carta/tarjeta.**
express (general delivery)	**urgente**
airmail	**vía aérea**
registered	**certificado**
I want to send a telegram to …	**Quisiera mandar un telegrama a …**
Can you get me this number in …?	**¿Puede comunicarme con este número en …?**

COMPLAINTS. Tourism is Spain's leading industry and the government takes complaints from tourists very seriously.

Hotels and restaurants: The great majority of disputes are attributable to misunderstandings and linguistic difficulties, and should not be exaggerated. As your host wants to keep both his reputation and his licence, you'll usually find him amenable to reason. In the event of a really serious and intractable problem, you may demand a complaint form *(hoja de reclamaciones)*, which all hotels and restaurants are required by law to have available. The original of this triplicate document should be sent to the regional office of the Ministry of Tourism; one copy stays with the establishment against which the complaint is registered, while the final copy remains in your hands as a record. Merely asking for a complaint form is usually enough of a threat to resolve most matters.

In the rare event of major obstruction, when it is not possible to call in the police, write directly to the Subsecretario del Turismo, Sección de Inspección y Reclamaciones:

Alcalá, 44, Madrid.

Bad merchandise and car repairs: Consumer protection is in its infancy in Spain. If you think you've been taken advantage of, all you can do is appeal to the proprietor.

In the event of gross abuse, take your complaint to the local tourist office. They're often able to sort out this kind of problem.

CONSULATES *(consulado)*. Most western European countries have consular offices in Barcelona. If you have trouble with the authorities or the police, consult your consulate for advice.

Canada: No consular office in Barcelona. Apply to the Consulate General, Edificio Goya, Calle Nuñez de Balboa, 35, Madrid; tel.: 2259119.

Great Britain*: Avenida del Generalísimo Franco, Edificio Torre de Barcelona, 13th floor, Barcelona; tel.: 3222151.

Eire: Gran Vía Carlos III, 94, Barcelona; tel.: 3309652.

U.S.A.: Vía Layetana, 33, Barcelona; tel.: 3199550.

South Africa: Plaza Duque de Medinaceli, 4, Barcelona; tel.: 3184258.

Where's the ... consulate?	**¿Dónde está el consulado**
British/American	**británico/americano?**
Canadian/Irish	**canadiense/irlandés?**
South African	**sudafricano?**
It's very urgent.	**Es muy urgente.**

---

* Also for citizens of Commonwealth countries.

C CONVERTER CHARTS. For fluid and distance measures, see page 110. Spain uses the metric system.

Temperature

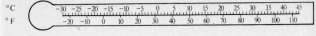

Length

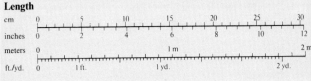

Weight

grams, ounces

COURTESIES. See also MEETING PEOPLE. Politeness and simple courtesies still matter in Spain. A handshake on greeting and leaving is normal. Always begin any conversation, whether with a friend, shop girl, taxi-driver, policeman or telephone operator with a *buenos días* (good morning) or *buenas tardes* (good afternoon). Always say *adiós* (goodbye or, oddly enough, hi/hallo, said at any time of the day) or, at night, *buenas noches* when leaving. *Por favor* (please) should begin all requests.

Finally, don't try to rush Spaniards. They have no appreciation for haste and consider it bad form when anyone pushes them on. Take your time. In Spain, there's plenty of it.

How do you do?	**Encantado de conocerle (conocerla** when addressing a women).
How are you?	**¿Como está usted?**
Very well, thank you.	**Muy bien, gracias.**

CRIME and THEFT. Spain's crime rate is low compared to the rest of the world. However, danger spots exist understandably where crowds collect—at *ferias, fiestas,* in buses and at markets, where purses are sometimes snatched from shopping baskets. Avoid taking valuables with you to the beach.

| I want to report a theft. My ticket/wallet/passport has been stolen. | **Quiero denunciar un robo. Me han robado el billete/ la cartera/el pasaporte.** |

DRIVING IS SPAIN

Entering Spain: To bring your car into Spain you will require:

International Driving Licence	Car registration papers	Green Card (an extension to your regular insurance policy, making it valid for foreign countries)
Recommended: a Spanish bail bond. If you injure somebody in an accident in Spain, you can be detained while the accident is being investigated. This bond will bail you out. Apply to your insurance company.		

A nationality sticker must be prominently displayed on the back of your car. If your car has seat belts, it's obligatory to use them. A red reflecting warning triangle is compulsory when driving on a motorway (expressway). Motorcycle riders and their passengers must wear crash helmets.

Driving conditions: Drive on the right. Pass on the left. Yield right of way to all traffic coming from the right. Spanish drivers tend to use their horn when passing other vehicles.

Main roads are adequate to very good and improving all the time. Secondary roads can be bumpy. The main danger of driving in Spain comes from impatience, especially on busy roads. A large percentage of accidents in Spain occur when passing, so take it easy. Wait until you have a long, unobstructed view.

Spanish truck and lorry drivers will often wave you on (by hand signal or by flashing their right directional signal) if it's clear ahead.

On country roads, beware of donkey and mule riders and horse-drawn carts. In villages, remember that the car only became a part of the Spanish way of life some 30 years ago; the villages aren't designed for them, and the older people are still not quite used to them. Drive with extra care to avoid children darting out of doorways and older folk strolling in the middle of the road, particularly after dark.

D **Parking:** Many towns charge a token fee for parking during working hours; the cities more. The attendants are often disabled, and it's usual to round off the price of the ticket upwards.

It is forbidden to park the car facing oncoming traffic.

Traffic police: Spanish roads are probably the best patrolled in all Europe. The men who do the patrolling are the motorcycle police of the Civil Guard *(Guardia Civil)*. They always ride in pairs and are always armed. They are extremely courteous at helping you find your way, are efficient with minor mechanical problems and go out of their way to help you if you have a breakdown. They are also tough on lawbreakers.

The most common offences include passing without flashing your lights, travelling too close to the car in front, and driving with a burned-out head- or rear-lamp. (Spanish law requires you to carry a set of spare bulbs at all times.)

Fuel and oil: Service stations, once sparsely dotted around the countryside, are now plentiful, particularly in tourist areas, but it's a good idea to keep an eye on the gauge in deserted areas.

All fuel is sold through the governement monopoly, *Campsa*, and is available in three grades, 90, 96 and 98 octane.

Fluid measures

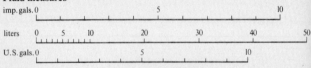

Distance

Breakdowns: Spanish garages are as efficient as any, but in tourist areas major repairs may take several days because of the heavy workload. Spare parts are readily available for all major makes of cars.

Road signs: Most road signs are the standard pictographs used throughout Europe. However, you may encounter these written signs:

¡Alto!	Stop!
Aparcamiento	Parking
Autopista (de peaje)	(Toll) motorway (expressway)
Ceda el paso	Give way (Yield)
Cruce peligroso	Dangerous crossroads
Cuidado	Caution
Despacio	Slow
Desviación	Diversion (Detour)
Peligro	Danger
Prohibido adelantar	No overtaking (passing)
Prohibido aparcar	No parking
Puesto de socorro	First-aid post

(International) Driving Licence	**carné de conducir (internacional)**
Car registration papers	**certificado de matrícula**
Green Card	**carta verde**

Are we on the right road for …?	**¿Es ésta la carretera hacia …?**
Fill her up, please, top grade.	**Llénelo, por favor, con super.**
Check the oil/tires/battery.	**Por favor, controle el aceite/ los neumáticos/la batería.**

I've had a breakdown.	**Mi coche se ha estropeado.**
There's been an accident.	**Ha habido un accidente.**

DRUGS. The Spanish police have no sympathy for narcotics of any sort, or their users. Possession can be considered as evidence of intent to traffic, and the minimum sentence is six months (and may go up to 20 years).

ELECTRIC CURRENT *(corriente eléctrica).* Today 220-volt A.C. is becoming standard, but older installations of 125 volts can still be found. Check before plugging in. If the voltage is 125, American appliances (e.g. razors) built for 60 cycles will run on 50-cycle European current, but more slowly.

If you have trouble with any of your appliances ask your hotel receptionist to recommend an *electricista.*

What's the voltage—125 or 220?	**¿Cuál es el voltaje—ciento veinticinco (125) o doscientos veinte (220)?**
an adaptor/a battery	**un adaptador/una pila**

E **EMERGENCIES.** Being thoroughly familiar with local conditions, your hotel receptionist or a taxi driver can be of great help. Depending on the nature of the emergency, refer to the separate entries in this section such as CONSULATES, MEDICAL CARE, POLICE, etc.

Though we hope you'll never need them, here are a few key words you might like to learn in advance:

Careful	**Cuidado**	Police	**Policía**
Fire	**Fuego**	Stop	**Deténgase**
Help	**Socorro**	Stop thief	**Al ladrón**

ENTRY and CUSTOMS FORMALITIES *(aduana)*. Citizens of Great Britain, the U.S.A., Canada and Eire need only a valid passport to visit Spain, and even this requirement is waived for the British, who may enter on the simplified Visitor's Passport. Though residents of Europe and North America aren't subject to any health requirements, visitors from further afield should check with a travel agent before departure in case inoculation certificates are called for.

Visitors from Australia, New Zealand and South Africa must have visas.

The following chart shows what main duty-free items you may take into Spain and, when returning home, into your own country:

Into:	Cigarettes	Cigars	Tobacco	Spirits	Wine
Spain*	200 (400)	50 (100)	250 g. (500 g.)	1 l. or	2 l.
Australia	200	or 250 g. or	250 g.	1 l. or	1 l.
Canada	200	and 50	and 900 g.	1.1 l. or	1.1 l.
Eire	200	or 50	or 250 g.	1 l. and	2 l.
N. Zealand	200	or 50	or ½ lb.	1 qt. and	1 qt.
S. Africa	400	and 50	and 250 g.	1 l. and	1 l.
U.K.	200	or 50	or 250 g.	1 l. and	2 l.
U.S.A.	200	and 100	and **	1 l. or	1 l.

* The figures in parentheses are for non-European visitors only.
**a reasonable quantity

You are also permitted personal clothing, jewellery and perfume, a still camera with accessories and five rolls of film, a cine-camera and five rolls of film, a pair of binoculars, etc. You may have to sign a guarantee that you won't sell certain items in your possession while in Spain, otherwise you may have to put up a deposit.

Currency restrictions: While there's no limit for the tourist on the import or export of foreign currencies or traveller's cheques, you can't bring in more than 100,000 pesetas, which should be declared to customs on arrival, or leave the country with more than 20,000 pesetas.

I've nothing to declare.	**No tengo nada que declarar.**
It's for my personal use.	**Es para mi uso personal.**

GUIDES and INTERPRETERS*. Any local tourist office will be able to help you find a qualified guide and/or interpreter. In Barcelona, there are special agencies for this kind of service:

Asociación de Informadores Turísticos, Pueblo Español, Torre del Este and

Guías e Intérpretes, Palacio del Congreso, Avda. María Cristina.

We'd like an English-speaking guide.	**Queremos un guía que hable inglés.**
I need an English interpreter.	**Necesito un intérprete de inglés.**

HAIRDRESSERS* *(peluquería)*/**BARBERS** *(barbería)*. Most large hotels have their own salons and the standard is generally very good. Prices are far lower in neighbourhood salons in the towns than in the resorts and chic hotels. For tipping suggestions, see TIPPING.

The following vocabulary will help:

I'd like a shampoo and set.	**Quiero lavado y marcado.**
I want a ...	**Quiero ...**
haircut	**un corte de pelo**
razor cut	**un corte a navaja**
blow-dry (brushing)	**un modelado**
permanent wave	**una permanente**
colour rinse/hair-dye	**un reflejo/un tinte**
manicure	**una manicura**
Don't cut it too short.	**No me lo corte mucho.**
A little more off (here).	**Un poco más (aquí).**

H　**HITCH-HIKING** *(auto-stop)*. In Spain, hitch-hiking is permitted everywhere. If you sleep out in the open, don't stay too close to camping and caravan (trailer) sites. Police passing the campsite may awaken you to check your identity.

Can you give me/us a lift to …?　　**¿Puede llevarme/llevarnos a …?**

HOTELS and ACCOMMODATION*. Spanish hotel prices are no longer government-controlled. Prices range from a few hundred pesetas per night for a simple but always clean double room in a village *fonda* (inn) to several thousand pesetas for a double in a luxurious five star hotel. Before the guest takes the room he fills out a form indicating the hotel category, room number and price and signs it. Breakfast and full board are not automatically included and only added to your bill when you have them.

When you check into your hotel you might have to leave your passport at the desk. Don't worry, you'll get it back in the morning.

Other forms of accommodation:

Hotel-Residencia and **Hostal:** Modest hotels, often family concerns, also graded by stars (one to three). Rates overlap with the lower range of hotels, e.g. a three-star *hostal* usually costs about the same as a two-star hotel.

Pensión: Boarding houses, graded one to three, with few amenities.

Fonda: Village inns, clean and unpretentious.

Parador: Of special interest to motorists, since usually located outside towns, often in very old or historic buildings. State-run, and reasonably priced, depending on facilities. Advance booking essential. There is one at Aiguablava on the Costa Brava, another inland at Vich.

Albergue: Wayside inns; stay limited to two nights. Also state-run.

Refugio: Mountain hunting lodges.

Albergue de Juventud: In the Costa Brava area there is one at Gerona and another in Barcelona. A youth-hostel membership card is required.

Residencia: When referred to as *hostal-residencia* or *hotel-residencia*, this term indicates a hotel without a restaurant.

a double/single room	**una habitación doble/sencilla**
with/without bath	**con/sin baño**
What's the rate per night?	**¿Cuál es el precio por noche?**

HOURS. Schedules here revolve around the siesta, one of the really great Spanish discoveries, aimed at keeping people out of the midday sun. The word has become universal; unfortunately, the custom hasn't. But when in Spain you should certainly try it. It is impolite to telephone, call at or otherwise disturb a household which you know observes the siesta ritual.

To accommodate the midday pause, most shops and offices open from 9 a.m. to 1 p.m. and then from 4 p.m. to 8 p.m. Restaurants start serving lunch about 1 p.m. and dinner between 8 and 10 p.m.

LANGUAGE. The official language of Spain, Castilian Spanish, is spoken throughout the Costa Brava and Catalonia. But Catalonia is a bilingual region and amongst themselves, Catalonians prefer to speak Catalan, a related Latin language. Since the death of Franco, there has been an enormous increase in the use of Catalan in both official and unofficial circles. This can cause confusion to the tourist looking for a street or monument; simple awareness that there may be this kind of problem, however, usually helps to circumvent it (see MAPS AND STREET NAMES).

Never dismiss Catalan as a mere dialect; the language boasts a lively and rich literary tradition, and the Catalans themselves—one of Spain's most intellectual and artistic peoples—are justifiably proud of it.

English, German and French are widely spoken in resort hotels and restaurants.

	Catalan	**Castilian**
Good morning	*Bon dia*	*Buenos días*
Good afternoon/ Good evening	*Bones tardes*	*Buenas tardes*
Good night	*Bona nit*	*Buenas noches*
Please	*Per favor*	*Por favor*
Thank you	*Gràcies*	*Gracias*
You're welcome	*De res*	*De nada*
Good-bye	*Adéu*	*Adiós*

The Berlitz phrase book, SPANISH FOR TRAVELLERS, covers most situations you are likely to encounter in your travels in Spain. The Berlitz-Spanish-English/English-Spanish pocket dictionary contains some 12,500 concepts, plus a menu-reader supplement.

Do you speak English?	**¿Habla usted inglés?**
I don't speak Spanish.	**No hablo español.**

L   **LAUNDRY and DRY-CLEANING.** Most hotels will handle laundry and dry-cleaning, but they'll usually charge more than a laundry *(lavandería)* or a dry-cleaners *(tintorería)*. For still greater savings, you can try a do-it-yourself launderette *(launderama)*.

Where's the nearest laundry/dry-cleaners?	**¿Dónde está la lavandería/ tintorería más cercana?**
I want these clothes cleaned/washed.	**Quiero que limpien/laven esta ropa.**
When will it be ready?	**¿Cuándo estará lista?**
I must have this for tomorrow morning.	**La necesito para mañana por la mañana.**

LOST PROPERTY. The first thing to do when you discover you've lost something is obviously to retrace your steps. If nothing comes to light, report the loss to the Municipal Police or the Guardia Civil.

I've lost my wallet/handbag/ passport.	**He perdido mi cartera/bolso/ pasaporte.**

M   **MAPS and STREET NAMES.** See also LANGUAGE. Since General Franco died, Spain has being undergoing a formidable upheaval in many domains. One manifestation is in the names of streets, many of which are being re-baptised, causing a tourist considerable confusion.

Places now sometimes have two names, an old and a new one that have no resemblance to each other; one may be Castilian, the other Catalan; one may pay honour to a hero of the Franco period, one a Catalan hero of history.

Maps cannot unfortunately keep up with this evolution, so, with the above in mind, it's worth enquiring immediately of a local inhabitant if you can't find a certain street you're looking for.

The maps in this guide were prepared by Falk-Verlag, which also publish a detailed map of Barcelona.

a street plan of ...	**un plano de la ciudad de ...**
a road map of this region	**un mapa de carretas de esta comarca**

MEDICAL CARE. By far the best solution, to be completely at ease, is to take out a special health insurance policy to cover the risk of illness and accident while on holiday. Your travel agent can also fix you up with Spanish tourist insurance (ASTES), but it is a slow-moving process. ASTES covers doctor's fees and clinical care.

Health care in the resort areas and in the major cities is good. Most of the major resort towns have private clinics; the cities and rural areas are served by municipal or provincial hospitals.

For minor ailments, visit the local first-aid post *(casa de socorro)*. Away from your hotel, don't hesitate to ask the police or a tourist information office for help. At your hotel, ask the staff to help you.

Farmacias (chemists' shops, drugstores) are usually open during normal shopping hours. After hours, at least one per town remains open all night, called *farmacia de guardia*, and its location is posted in the window of all other *farmacias*.

Where's the nearest (all-night) pharmacy?	**¿Dónde está la farmacia (de guardia) más cercana?**
I need a doctor/dentist.	**Necesito un médico/dentista.**
I've a pain here.	**Me duele aquí.**
sunburn	**quemadura de sol**
sunstroke	**una isolación**
a fever	**fiebre**
an upset stomach	**molestias de estómago**
insect bite	**una picadura de insecto**

MEETING PEOPLE. The Spanish, as a whole, are one the world's most open and hospitable peoples, easy to talk to and approach, generous to a fault.

You might on occasions find the noise-level of a conversation somewhat deafening. What you perhaps take for a quarrel is more often than not simply news and gossip being transmitted... passionately.

The Spanish have their own pace. Not only is it bad manners to try to rush them, but unproductive as well.

Outrageous flattery and persistence from complete strangers is the local tactic on the Costa Brava, a harmless one. But if you're firm and aloof, your admirer will move off.

MONEY MATTERS

Currency: The monetary unit of Spain is the *peseta* (abbreviated *pta.*), which technically is divided into 100 *céntimos*.

Coins: 1, 5, 25 and 50 pesetas.

Banknotes: 100, 500, 1,000 and 5,000 pesetas.

A 5-peseta coin is traditionally called a *duro*, so if someone should quote a price as 10 duros, he means 50 pesetas. For currency restrictions, see ENTRY AND CUSTOMS FORMALITIES.

M　**Banks** are open from 9 a.m. to 2 p.m. Monday to Friday (Saturday 9 a.m. to 1 p.m.) in summer. In winter 9 a.m. to 1 p.m. Monday–Saturday. All banks are closed on Sundays and holidays—and watch out for those obscure holidays which occur so frequently in Spain!

Outside normal banking hours, many travel agencies, major hotels and other businesses displaying a *cambio* sign will change foreign currency into pesetas. The exchange rate is less favourable than in the banks. Banks and exchange offices pay slightly more for traveller's cheques than for cash. Always take your passport with you for identification when you go to exchange money.

Credit cards: The credit-card system is a new concept to Spain. Diner's Club and American Express are the most widely accepted cards. Although many hotels, restaurants and tourist-related businesses accept credit cards, Spaniards place much more trust in cash.

Eurocheques are accepted in Spain.

Traveller's cheques: In tourist areas, shops and all banks, hotels and travel agencies accept them, though you are likely to get a better rate of exchange at a national or regional bank. Remember always to take your passport along if you expect to cash a traveller's cheque.

Paying cash: Although many shops and bars will accept payment in sterling or dollars, you're best off paying in pesetas. Shops will give you less than the bank rate for foreign currency.

Prices: Inflation is painful in Spain, yet the cost of living remains somewhat lower than in most other European countries and North America.

How much your holiday will cost depends upon your budget and taste, but you still don't need a lot of money to have a good time in Spain.

Some prices are listed on page 101 to give you an idea of what things cost.

Where's the nearest bank/ currency exchange office?	**¿Dónde está el banco/la oficina de cambio más cercana?**
I want to change some pounds/ dollars.	**Quiero cambiar libras/dólares.**
Do you accept traveller's cheques?	**¿Acepta usted cheques de viaje?**
Can I pay with this credit card?	**¿Puedo pagar con esta tarjeta de crédito?**
How much is that?	**¿Cuánto es?**

MOSQUITOES. With the occasional exception there are rarely more than a few mosquitoes at a given time, but they survive the year round, and just one can ruin a night's sleep. Few hotels, flats or villas—anywhere on the Mediterranean—have mosquito-proofed windows. Bring your own anti-mosquito devices, whether nets, buzzers, lotions, sprays or incense-type coils that burn all night.

NEWSPAPERS and MAGAZINES *(periódico; revista).* In major tourist areas you can buy most European and British newspapers and magazines on the day of publication. U.S. magazines are available, as well as the Paris-based *International Herald Tribune.*

The *Iberian Daily Sun*, an English-language national daily newspaper, is available on the Costa Brava, as is *Lookout, the Magazine About Spain*, a glossy monthly.

Have you any English-language newspapers?	**¿Tienen periódicos en inglés?**

PHOTOGRAPHY. All popular film makes and sizes are available in Spain, though 6×6 film can be found in 120 rolls but not 220 rolls. Prices are generally higher than in the rest of Europe or North America, so it is advisable to bring a good stock. Polaroid film is expensive.

Photo shops in major resorts can develop and print black and white or colour film in 24 to 48 hours at reasonable prices; but films mailed to Agfa or Kodak in Madrid probably won't return for at least a week.

The Spanish films, *Negra* and *Valca* in black and white, and *Negracolor* in colour, are of good quality and cheaper than the internationally known brands.

Photo shops sell lead-coated plastic bags which protect films from X-rays at airport security checkpoints.

I'd like a film for this camera.	**Quisiera un carrete para esta máquina.**
a black-and-white film	**un carrete en blanco y negro**
a colour-slide film	**un carrete de diapositivas**
a film for colour pictures	**un carrete para película en color**
35-mm film	**un carrete treinta y cinco**
super-8	**super ocho**
How long will it take to develop (and print) this film?	**¿Cuánto tardará en revelar (y sacar copias de) este carrete?**
May I take a picture?	**¿Puedo sacar una foto?**

P **POLICE** *(policía)*. There are three police forces in Spain. The most famous, and best recognized, are the *Guardia Civil* (Civil Guard), who wear those distinctive patent-leather hats. Each sizeable town also has *Policía Municipal* (municipal police), who wear blue or grey uniforms with badges. The third unit, the *Policía Nacional*, a national anti-crime unit, can be recognized by their brown uniforms and black berets. Actually, all three forces are armed.

If you need police assistance, you can call on any one of the three.

Where's the nearest police station?	**¿Dónde está la comisaría más cercana?**

PUBLIC HOLIDAYS *(fiesta)*

January 1	*Año Nuevo*	New Year's Day
January 6	*Epifanía*	Epiphany
May 1	*Día del Trabajo*	Labour Day
July 25	*Santiago Apóstol*	St. James' Day
August 15	*Asunción*	Assumption
October 12	*Día de la Hispanidad*	Discovery of America Day (Columbus Day)
December 8	*Inmaculada Concepción*	Immaculate Conception
December 25	*Navidad*	Christmas Day
Movable dates:	*Jueves Santo*	Maundy Thursday (afternoon only)
	Viernes Santo	Good Friday
	Corpus Christi	Corpus Christi

These are only the national holidays of Spain. There are many special holidays for different branches of the economy or different regions. Consult the tourist office where you are staying.

Are you open tomorrow?	**¿Está abierto mañana?**

R **RADIO and TV** *(radio; televisión)*. Occasional English-language broadcasts can be picked up from Majorca. Up-to-date details can be supplied by tourist-information offices. English broadcasts can also be picked up on the BBC World Service with medium-wave transistors.

RELIGIOUS SERVICES *(servicio religioso)*. In Costa Brava resort
towns, religious services in English are held only occasionally. English-
language mass is said at Sta. Cristina Church in Lloret. In Barcelona, services are conducted in English on Sundays at the following
churches:

Catholic: Parroquia de Santa María de la Bonanova, Plaza de la Bonanova, 12 (confessions are heard in English in Barcelona Cathedral on
Sundays).

Protestant: St. George's Anglican Church, San Juan Bautista de la
Salle, 41 (near Plaza de la Bonanova).

Jewish: The synagogue is located at Calle Porvenir, 24.

What time is mass/the service?	**¿A qué hora es la misa/el culto?**
Is it in English?	**¿Es en inglés?**

TIME DIFFERENCES. Spanish time coincides with most of Western
Europe—Greenwich Mean Time plus one hour. In spring, another
hour is added for Daylight Saving Time (Summer Time). If your
country does the same, the difference remains constant most of the
year.

Summer Time chart:

New York	London	**Madrid**	Jo'burg	Sydney	Auckland
6 a.m.	11 a.m.	**noon**	1 p.m.	8 p.m.	10 p.m.

What time is it?   **¿Qué hora es?**

TIPPING. Since a service charge is included in hotels and restaurant
bills, tipping is not obligatory. However, it's appropriate to tip porters,
bellboys, etc. for their efforts. Follow the chart below for rough guide-
lines.

Hotel porter, per bag	25 ptas.
Bellboy, errand	50 ptas.
Maid, per week	100 ptas.
Doorman, hails cab	25 ptas.

Waiter	10–12%, if service not incl.
Taxi driver	10%
Filling station attendant	25 ptas., optional
Tourist guide	10%
Hairdresser	10%
Cinema usher	10–15 ptas.
Bullfight usher	10–15 ptas.
Lavatory attendant	10–15 ptas.

TOILETS. There are many expressions for "toilets" in Spanish: *aseos*, *servicios*, *W.C.*, *water* and *retretes*. The first two terms are the more common.

Public toilets are to be found in most large Spanish towns, but rarely in villages. However, just about every bar and restaurant has a toilet available for public use. It's considered polite to buy a coffee or a glass of wine if you drop in specifically to use the conveniences.

Where are the toilets?   **¿Dónde están los servicios?**

TOURIST-INFORMATION OFFICES *(oficina de turismo)*. Spanish National Tourist Offices are maintained in many countries throughout the world:

Canada: 60 Bloor St. West, Suite 201, Toronto, Ont. M4W-IAI; tel.: (416) 961-3131

United Kingdom: 57–58, St. James St., London SW 1A; tel. (01) 4990901.

U.S.A.: 845 N. Michigan Ave., Chicago IL 60611; tel.: (312) 944-0215.
665 5th Ave. New York, N.Y. 10017; tel.: (212) 759-8822.
Casa del Hidalgo, Hypolita & St. George Streets, St. Augustine, FL 31084; tel.: (904) 829-6460.
3160 Lyon St., San Francisco, CA 94108; tel.: (415) 346-8100.

These offices will supply you with a wide range of colourful and informative brochures and maps in English on the various towns and regions in Spain. They will also let you consult a copy of the master directory of hotels in Spain, listing all facilities and prices.

All major cities and resorts in Spain have tourist-information offices. Normal hours: 10 a.m.–1 p.m. and 4–7.30 p.m.

Where is the tourist office?	**¿Dónde está la oficina de turismo?**

TRANSPORT

Bus services. The Costa Brava, Gerona, Barcelona and inland towns of Catalonia are well served by several private bus companies. Destinations are clearly marked on the front of the bus. Remember that when taking a local bus, you normally enter by the back door and get out by the front door.

Buses are cheaper than trains, and a two-way bus ticket will work out cheaper than a travel-agency tour.

Taxis* *(taxi).* Spanish taxis are amongst the cheapest in Europe. Gerona and Barcelona taxis have meters, but in villages along the rest of the coast they don't, so it's a good idea to check the fare before you get in. If you take a long trip—for example between two villages—you will be charged a two-way fare whether you make the return journey or not.

Trains. While local trains are very slow, stopping at almost all stations, long-distance services, especially the *Talgo* and *Ter*, are fast and punctual. First-class coaches are comfortable; second-class, adequate. There is also a third class on some trains—not very comfortable, but cheap. Tickets can be purchased at travel agencies as well as at railway stations *(estación de ferrocarril).* Seat reservations are recommended.

Talgo, Ter	Luxury diesel, first and second classes; supplementary charge over regular fare
Expreso, Rápido	Long-distance expresses, stopping at main stations only
Omnibus, Tranvía, Automotor	Local trains, with frequent stops
coche cama	Sleeping-car with 1-, 2- or 3-bed compartments, washing facilities
coche comedor	Dining-car

T		
	litera	Sleeping-berth car *(couchette)* with blankets, sheets and pillows
	furgón de equipajes	Luggage van (baggage car); only registered luggage permitted

When's the best train to …?	**¿Cuál es el mejor tren para …?**
single (one-way)	**ida**
return (round-trip)	**ida y vuelta**
first/second/third class	**primera/segunda/tercera clase**
I'd like to make seat reservations.	**Quiero reservar asientos.**

W   **WATER** *(agua).* When Spaniards drink water, it is almost invariably bottled water, rather than from the tap. It is quite common to order water brought to one's room. If you're particularly sensitive to water, watch out, too, for the ice cubes in drinks. Water varies enormously in taste and quality, and the bottled variety is good, pure and cheap.

a bottle of mineral water	**una botella de agua mineral**
fizzy (carbonated)	**con gas**
still	**sin gas**
Is this drinking water?	**¿El agua es potable?**

DAYS OF THE WEEK

DAYS

Sunday	**domingo**	Wednesday	**miércoles**
Monday	**lunes**	Thursday	**jueves**
Tuesday	**martes**	Friday	**viernes**
		Saturday	**sábado**

MONTHS

January	**enero**	July	**julio**
February	**febrero**	August	**agosto**
March	**marzo**	September	**septiembre**
April	**abril**	October	**octubre**
May	**mayo**	November	**noviembre**
June	**junio**	December	**diciembre**

SOME USEFUL EXPRESSIONS

yes/no	**sí/no**
please/thank you	**por favor/gracias**
excuse me/you're welcome	**perdone/de nada**
where/when/how	**dónde/cuándo/cómo**
how long/how far	**cuánto tiempo/a qué distancia**
yesterday/today/tomorrow	**ayer/hoy/mañana**
day/week/month/year	**día/semana/mes/año**
left/right	**izquierda/derecha**
up/down	**arriba/abajo**
good/bad	**bueno/malo**
big/small	**grande/pequeño**
cheap/expensive	**barato/caro**
hot/cold	**caliente/frío**
old/new	**viejo/nuevo**
open/closed	**abierto/cerrado**
here/there	**aquí/allí**
free (vacant)/occupied	**libre/ocupado**
early/late	**temprano/tarde**
easy/difficult	**fácil/difícil**
Does anyone here speak English?	**¿Hay alguien aquí que hable inglés?**
What does this mean?	**¿Qué quiere decir esto?**
I don't understand.	**No comprendo.**
Please write it down.	**Por favor, escríbalo.**
Is there an admission charge?	**¿Se debe pagar la entrada?**
Waiter!/Waitress!	**¡Camarero!/¡Camarera!**
I'd like …	**Quisiera …**
How much is that?	**¿Cuánto es?**
Have you something less expensive?	**¿Tiene algo más barato?**
Help me, please.	**Ayúdeme, por favor.**
Get a doctor, quickly.	**¡Llamen a un médico, rápidamente!**

Index

An asterisk (*) next to a page number indicates a map reference. For index to Practical Information, see p. 102.

INDEX

2/81 RV